THE MINISTRY LIFE

101 TIPS FOR NEW MINISTERS

Smyth & Helwys Publishing, Inc.
6316 Peake Road
Macon, Georgia 31210-3960
1-800-747-3016
©2013 by John Killinger
All rights reserved.
Printed in the United States of America.

The paper used in this publication meets the minimum requirements of
American National Standard for Information Sciences—
Permanence of Paper for Printed Library Materials.
ANSI Z39.48–1984. (alk. paper)

Library of Congress Cataloging-in-Publication Data

CIP information on file

The *Ministry Life*

101 Tips *for* New Ministers

John Killinger

Also by John Killinger

I happily dedicate this book

to my young cousin

Rodney Drew Weseman

as he steps forth

to become a servant

of Christ

Acknowledgments

No book is ever solely the product of the author whose name it bears, for all writers owe their views of everything to many others, from parents and teachers at life's beginning to the doctors and nurses who tend us at the end. Of the countless people who in one way or another contributed to the existence of this book, I cheerfully mention some:

The members of my various churches through the years—Bronston Baptist Church in Bronston, Kentucky; Poplar Grove Baptist Church in Rockcastle County, Kentucky; Union Baptist Church in North Reading, Massachusetts; Raritan Valley Baptist Church in Edison, New Jersey; First Presbyterian Church in Lynchburg, Virginia; The First Congregational Church of Los Angeles; The Little Stone Church on Mackinac Island, Michigan; and Marble Collegiate Church in New York City. You good people taught me far more about being a pastor than all my professors in divinity school combined!

Keith Gammons, the publisher and executive vice president of Smyth & Helwys, who has always encouraged me to show him what I was working on, and Leslie Andres, my genial and thoughtful editor, who has been a great help and a joy to work with. Thank you both for everything!

My wife, Anne, who has been my dearest and most reliable critic through all my pastorates, and our son Eric, who himself pastored three churches before becoming a publisher and continues to share with dad his deep insights about life and the church and his invaluable expertise on computers. I love you both!

My many, many colleagues in ministry, some of whom have been good enough to share their wisdom with us in the final section of this book. Your contributions have made this a far richer book than I could have ever made it alone!

Contents

**Ten Tips Each from Other Ministers: Advice from Those
Who Have Been There**

Introduction

There is a lot of truth in the adage, "Any fool can make a sermon, but only God can make a minister." After more than fifty years in the ministry, I have to confess that I have often felt more like a fool than a minister.

But I did learn a few things along the way and made a lot of friends in the ministry who also learned a few things. These insights are what I'm jotting down in this book.

What I am setting down—101 tips or suggestions—is by no means the sum total of what one needs to become a minister. For that, every minister is on his or her own. But my hope is that these short-cuts will help new, unseasoned ministers find their way a little more easily and quickly than they might have done otherwise.

These tips are probably not without error. Sometimes we all feel foolish, doubting our ability to become the minister God calls us to be. Sometimes we find that even our best thoughts are misdirected or compounded by ignorance. But on the whole, there is a lot of wisdom in these pages. Given enough years and enough mistakes along the way, the reader would surely discover most of these for him- or herself, but perhaps this book can speed the process along to help you create a more productive, effective, and enjoyable ministry today.

These tips aren't meant to be bedtime reading. They can be picked up for a moment at any time and put down until another moment presents itself. The idea is to read them until you find one that really resonates with you or your situation. Then lay the book aside and mull it over until you figure out how to incorporate it into your own wisdom and behavior. Pick up the book again at another time and discover another useful tip. And so on, until you've made your way through the book.

You won't be a better preacher because you've read the book (although there are some valuable tips about preaching herein), and you won't be a greater theologian. But the chances are you will learn some things or discover some pointers that will make you review your own practices, and that alone will be worth the time it takes to leaf through the book.

As Socrates said, the unexamined life is not worth living. That's doubly true of the minister's life.

It is only as we reflect on our own experiences—and sift them together with the thoughts and experiences of other ministers—that we begin to understand whether we've really found the knack of being servants of God.

These tips, I hope, will aid you in doing that.

1

Don't ever go into a pastoral situation thinking you have to do everything yourself.

You don't and you can't. Life is too big and the ministry is too complex for you to be able to manage it all on your own.

People are difficult, and so is institutional management.

Think of it this way: You are a pastor. A pastor is a shepherd. A shepherd can scout the terrain and go ahead of the sheep and try to keep them out of trouble, but the shepherd cannot eat for the sheep or digest what they eat or grow their wool for them. They must do that for themselves.

You can provide a spiritual model for your people, but you cannot make them follow it.

You can preach the gospel for them, but you cannot make them hear it.

You can make suggestions about the way Christian organizations should comport themselves in the world, but you cannot make your church, its officers, or its members behave the way you'd like them to.

There will come a time, perhaps years after you've started your ministry, when you will wonder, *Why have I ever bothered to preach and teach as I have? People go right on being the way they were as if I hadn't ever said a word!*

But remember that it isn't your job to live their lives or reorganize the church for them. Your job is to be faithful to your calling as a preacher and pastor, which means letting your light shine when everybody else's has gone out (or seems to have done so) and letting it shine until God's kingdom comes, if necessary.

In Jan Karon's novel *A New Song* (Penguin, 2000), Father Timothy, the rector of all the Mitford stories, yearns to go back to the aid of some people in his old pastorate. His wife tells him he always wants to help everybody and fix everything.

He says he knows he does, but he can't help it.

She reminds him of a sign she keeps over her drawing board. It says, "Don't feel totally, personally, irrevocably responsible for everything. That's my job. Signed, God."

2

Love everybody in your pastorate, especially your enemies.

It won't be easy. Some of those people are real stinkers. Some have even made a career out of being stinkers. It's almost as if they feel a bounden duty to be stinkers.

But they are your parishioners, and, as such, they are entitled to your love and care. You are obligated, perhaps more than anybody else in the world except maybe their mothers, to try to understand them and what makes them the way they are, and then to give them the kind of therapy only a pastor can give.

You will convert a few of them during your ministry in their church, but some will never be converted. They are going to heaven as stinkers, and God will have to deal with them there.

But for now, they are your problem and you must try to love them.

You may be very surprised some day, after you have moved on to another church, to look back and remember some of these folks with great fondness. It's true. Many ministers find this to be the case. It seems contrary to all rules and reason, but the sense of engagement you've had with these people will endear them to you long after you have forgotten most of the "ordinary" members in your flock.

Not only that, but someday when you go back to your old church for a special occasion, such as a reunion or a big anniversary celebration, you will find that some of the folks who gave you the most trouble will be the ones who squeeze you the hardest and profess the most love for you.

Think of old Jacob wrestling with that angel in the shallows of the Jabbok. He was forever indebted to that dark stranger who fought with him most of the night. The struggle left him wounded in the thigh, and he walked with a limp for the rest of his life. But he never forgot the stranger and recalled him as an angel, a messenger of God.

Some of your worst enemies in the church are actually messengers of God. You'll find that hard to believe sometimes, but it's true. They will remind you of who you really are and what God really wants of you in your pastorate.

So don't dismiss them out of hand, as if they're the scourge of the earth. They're not. They are some of God's misbehaving children, that's all. And you're sent to their parish to remind them of that for a while.

Consider it an honor!

3

Take the sunshine with you wherever you go, not the clouds.

People respond to a happy person, not a gloomy one.

There will be days when you feel like stepping on your lower lip, you're so weighed down with cares and burdens of every kind. But don't let it show to your parishioners. They have the right to see you in the very best light, and to let that light transform their dreary lives into something kinder, gentler, and better.

One of the early church Fathers, describing Moses when he came down from the mount to speak to the Israelites, said he had "a bloom of glory" on his face. And if you spend time with God every day, you ought to develop such a bloom on your own countenance.

That's what your people want to see when you come around because they know it will change their lives, even if only ever so slightly.

It's now officially true. Two researchers, Dr. Nicholas Christakis and Dr. James Fowler of the University of California at San Diego, have said so in an article in the *British Medical Journal* (December 2008): happiness is like a virus that spreads from person to person. It even spreads beyond its original source to include other people who didn't come near the person who started it.

So be the person in your parish who starts this contagion of joy.

If the parson can't do it, who can?

4

Pay attention to the little things.

They may not seem important in and of themselves, but they are the multiple building blocks of your ministry.

Lewis Weeks, the former president of Union Theological Seminary in Richmond, Virginia, wrote about a certain church whose congregation placed their worship bulletins in the offering plates every Sunday with all the typos boldly circled.

Little things, little errors, little faux pas, little snafus. And no less a wise man than Benjamin Franklin reminded us that a lot of little leaks will sink a ship as fast as one big one.

This doesn't mean that the pastor should micromanage everything. That would be a hell of a responsibility (read as a pun or not). The pastor as Pecksniff isn't a pretty picture.

What it does mean is that a regular patrol of the grounds is required to be sure the sentinels are alert and that people of quality and concern are at the controls in all areas of the church's life, from maintenance to education. It means spot-checks to be sure that safeguards are in place and that people are doing their various duties in all relevant areas. It means having someone—a faithful secretary, a great volunteer, a vigilant deacon—tending to the nuts and bolts so that the wings don't fall off when the church picks up speed while taxiing down the runway.

What were Jesus' words? "Well done, thou good and faithful servant. You have been faithful over a few things, I will make you master over many" (Matt 25:23).

5

Keep your eye on the big things.

Don't let the management of paperclips and memoranda divert you from the really big items on the pastor's agenda, such as great worship services, faithful pastoral care, a dependable output of true and worthy sermons, a fine educational program, a steady hand on the helm to keep the church on course for the kingdom, and a fine attention to the ideas and programs that shape people's lives for deeper thinking and higher living.

Every pastor is tempted, after a few months on the job, to relax and go with the flow. That sounds okay, especially if the flow is in the right direction. But drifting can be a dangerous thing, for what it really means is that no one is in charge and you aren't actually going anywhere that matters.

Once, in Holland, my wife and I were on a boat on the Zuyder Zee that lost its power and began to drift toward shallow waters. Afterward, the captain admitted his fear of what would have happened if a passing ship hadn't thrown us a line and towed us out. "I was afraid," he said, "that we would get beyond rescue. Then I'm not sure what would have happened to us."

The same is true of churches that are allowed to float along without any commitment to the important things on every church's agenda. Eventually they drift into the shallow places where their rescue is no longer simple or easy.

So make a point of doing frequent reviews of your church's situation. Ask hard questions about where you're going and what steps you're taking to get there. Score yourself and the church on the really big items on the agenda and then act to raise the scores in the most crucial areas.

Ask yourself, *Am I making a real difference here?* If the answer is no, then it may be time for the church to select a new leader.

Preach the sermons you would like to hear.

It will, of course, be tempting to preach the sermons you think are especially good or attention-getting, the ones that will end up in somebody's collection of great sermons one day. But resist this temptation at all costs, for succumbing to it will eventually make you a redundant preacher and a hireling shepherd.

Put yourself in the place of some of the people in your congregation: the clerk who stands on her feet all day even though she's past sixty, the couple whose son recently left for military service, the retired school teacher who just buried his wife, the teenager who got arrested on a DUI charge, the banker who lost his job, the woman who was released from prison a few weeks ago.

A psychiatrist faces a needy person every time he or she enters the counseling room. A minister faces dozens or hundreds of them every time he or she approaches the pulpit.

Remember this, and preach to people's needs. Preach to your own needs, if you don't know the needs of others. Sit down and analyze what it is you'd like to hear if you were going to church somewhere else next Sunday. Are you nervous about your job? Unhappy about the economy? Uncertain about your faith? Strained in your personal relationships? Exhausted from overwork? Then frame sermons that will address these common problems.

You can be sure that if you take good aim at yourself, you will hit a lot of other people with your shot.

Mickey Spillane, the originator of the hard-boiled detective novel, once said that he wrote the kind of books he'd like to read.

That's what preachers ought to do—preach the kinds of sermons they would like to hear, were they in the pew and not in the pulpit.

No more "Saturday night specials." No more generic, one-size-fits-all sermons. No more "nice little homilies." But honest-to-goodness sermons that are forged out of the confrontation of the gospel with the facts of life. The hard facts, not the easy ones. The ones that can make even a preacher weep at the frailty of the human situation and the wonder of the gospel!

Care about the little children as if they were the most important members of your congregation.

In a way, they are. They are the future of the church, and what they learn from you and other adults now will in large measure determine what they think and believe later.

Jesus chided his disciples for wanting to ignore children in favor of adults, and he told them not to forbid the children from thronging around him. He knew how important they would be. Many of them doubtless became faithful church members before many years had elapsed.

I remember a thoughtful pastor who confessed to "the worst thing" he'd ever done in his ministry. It was on a Sunday morning, and his church had issued an invitation for converts and people wanting to join the church. Three people came forward. One was a new banker in town whom the minister had called on and was anxious to have join his church. Another was the banker's wife. The third was a small boy, about eight or nine years old.

"God forgive me," said the pastor in tortured remembrance, "I really made over the banker and his wife, and all but ignored the boy. Finally, after a fulsome introduction of the couple, during which I made sure people knew I had been on the job to recruit them, I realized the boy had come forward too, and I turned and welcomed him."

He hoped not too many people noticed the difference in his welcome of the adults compared to that of the child, but he said *he* knew, and he felt awful about it.

Well, he should!

Don't make the same mistake. Take time for the children. Listen to them, visit with them, make over them. Above all, let them know you love them. In some cases, your love will be the only love they really get. I felt that way as a boy. It's probably the reason I'm in the ministry today.

8

Don't forget to really pray.

That's "really" as in actually, in fact, devoting real time to it, letting it inform who you are and how you live.

Ministers pray all the time. I know that. But so much of our praying is perfunctory—prayers to open the service, prayers to introduce meetings, prayers over meals, prayers for civic affairs, prayers for ball games, prayers for people who come for counseling.

That's all well and good. Life ought to be punctuated by good prayers.

But I'm talking here about the prayer line that keeps you in touch with God and that challenges your puny existence, your prejudiced way of looking at things, your routine, ordinary way of getting by from day to day. I'm talking deep prayer, the kind where you put yourself in front of God and wait for orders or wait to be chided for what's been wrong in your approach to things or wait to be held and loved and blessed.

I'm partial to Mother Teresa's description of what she did when she prayed. A reporter once asked her what it was like. What did she say to God when she prayed?

"Nothing," she said. "I just listen."

"Oh?" said the reporter. "And what does God say to you?"

"Nothing," she said again. "He just listens too."

Two listeners, one divine and one human, just being there for one another. Not doing anything. Not asking for anything. Not exchanging any burdens. Just listening. Just being there. Just sharing the space.

How that kind of prayer irradiates the life of the one praying! How it changes everything, from the way we think about our lives and our work to the way we feel about God.

Every pastor gets into deep and troubled water at times. The only way to ride out those times is to have a good rope and a strong anchor. And only the pastor who knows how to pray, to truly pray and be with God, has such a rope and such an anchor.

9

Read, read, read, as though your intellectual and spiritual life depended on it.

Too many pastors think that when they receive their diplomas from seminary it's time to put away the books and get down to real work. But that's a mistake. Reading is real work. Even if you like to do it, it's still real work. It's the way you continue to grow in life and ministry, to expand your consciousness, sand off the rough edges, and become a more effective minister.

Old Alexander Whyte, the Edinburgh minister, used to advise his students to sell their beds, if they had to, in order to buy books. He knew what he was talking about. He understood that reading books was the only way they would grow into the ministers God had called them to be.

George A. Buttrick, the great minister at Madison Avenue Presbyterian Church in New York, who later became the beloved dean of the chapel at Harvard University, read two books a week. He said he couldn't stay alive as a pastor unless he did. And still he found time to write several important books and edit the famous Interpreter's Bible series of commentaries.

Don't only read the books you're expected to read—the Christian classics, the latest devotional book, books that will feed your sermons. Read the books that will double or triple your knowledge in some field that has been foreign to you. Read about physics, geology, weather, astronomy, psychology. Read the great novels and poetry of the world. Read about other religions.

That's how you'll manage to leapfrog over the person you once were and astound yourself, halfway through your ministry, by how much more knowledgeable you are now than when you started. That's also how you'll be able to pepper your sermons with allusions and illustrations that will be fresh and compelling to your congregation, especially the readers and thinkers within it.

Paul Scherer, one of my own mentors in the faith, always read the daily paper standing up. He said he didn't want to become mentally lazy by enjoying only the writings of journalists who made it easy for their readers. He wanted to do his hard reading sitting down with a thick book and a pen in his hand to mark it up as he read.

You don't want to become a snob, though, always dropping allusions to the great books you've read. The trick is to do the reading and know the stuff but then to guard against talking about it all the time.

As someone advised me when I was a young minister, "Read Plato all week and preach to field hands on Sunday."

It's a little bit like wearing a hair shirt under your linen robe, which G. K. Chesterton once said gives you the advantage of learning humility while letting others enjoy the beauty of your appearance.

Never allow routines, however important they may be, to interfere with your doing the real work of a pastor.

Jacques Barzun, the great Columbia professor, said in *Teacher in America* that the reason few professors ever rise to the heights of their profession is because they enjoy the routines too much. Suppose one teaches a class until eleven o'clock, then returns to his office, he said. It's still an hour till lunch. He really ought to get to work on that important book he has thought of writing. He looks at his watch and thinks, *I suppose I should go to the library.* Then he remembers and says, "Thank God, there's a meeting—and it counts as work!"

So he rushes off to the meeting, content with the ordinary things he will think and say there, and never gets around to writing his book.

A truly good pastor is one who tends to the necessary work of the day—the meetings, calls, memos, and letters—but doesn't allow them to obscure the greater work that needs to be done, such as researching an important sermon, meeting with a hard-boiled critic who is bound to be unpleasant, consulting with some great visionary in the community, or drafting the overall plans for a significant new program.

No farmer ever raised a good crop without first plowing a deep furrow. And no minister ever led a church to the peaks of its real possibilities without putting in his or her time at the art of real leadership.

One fine minister I knew had a church member who owned a motel with balconies overlooking a little stream. By arrangement with that member, he used to go to the motel one morning a week, while the maids were making up the rooms, and sit on a balcony and simply *think* about his ministry and what he was or wasn't doing to fulfill it. It was his way of rising above the ephemera that easily drown out any kind of working life and keeping himself on track toward a truly productive and meaningful ministry.

It practically guaranteed that he would be an *extra*ordinary pastor.

Work diligently and excitedly on your liturgical prayers.

Spending hours laboring over a few sentences you will offer in prayer on a Sunday morning doesn't sound like glamorous work. Why, you probably think, especially if you come from a spirit-filled tradition, no minister should waste time working on public prayers. Won't the Holy Spirit give you what you need to say?

I once heard Paul Tillich, the eminent theologian, tell about a young minister named Hans who vowed not to prepare his prayers in advance, regardless of how much his teachers insisted that he should. He got up in the pulpit on the first Sunday in his new parish, bowed his head, and waited for the Spirit to speak to him.

"And what did the Spirit say?" a friend asked later.

Hans shook his head sadly. "He said, 'Hans, you're a damn fool!'"

It is one thing to offer one's helplessness to God in private prayer. It is quite another thing, charged with leading public prayers, to stumble around in one's language like a drunken barfly and end up repeating old clichéd prayers everybody has heard for years.

A good liturgical prayer—one well crafted and expressive of the deepest emotional, sociological, and theological concerns of the congregants—is like a rare gem whose facets, turned in the light, exhibit a radiance that captivates and inspires the worshipers.

George Buttrick was an extraordinary preacher, and he advised fellow preachers to allow an hour's preparation time for every minute spent delivering a sermon. Yet he believed so strongly in the importance of fine prayers that he often said to his students, "If you have time to spend only on your prayers or only on your sermon, there should be no question about it. Spend it on your prayers!"

Novice ministers are advised to secure copies of some of the finest collections of prayers available, such as John Baillie's *A Diary of Private Prayer* (Touchstone, 1996) and Samuel H. Miller's *Prayers for Daily Use* (Harper, 1957), and steep themselves in the deep concerns and manners of expression in those oblations until offering similar prayers for the congregation becomes second nature. There can be no better investment than this in the church's worship and spiritual welfare.

Note

1. Some of these great prayer classics are hard to find, but prayers inspired by them may be found in my three volumes of pulpit prayers published by Abingdon Press: *Lost in Wonder, Love & Praise* (2001), *Enter Every Trembling Heart* (2002), and *God's People at Prayer* (2006).

Take time off to just "be human" and do some of the foolish, unprofitable things human beings do.

Of course you are a minister of God, charged with doing great things in the world. But if you remember only that, your days will be filled with important charges and little else, and you will become dull, stuffy, and out of touch with the beauty of humanity.

St. Paul was right, in the letter to the Corinthians, to say that we have the treasure of the gospel in earthen vessels. Part of the glory and mystique of the gospel is that it is encased in scarred and vulnerable pottery. Some of the greatest ministers of the church have also been among the humblest and most approachable, able to laugh with children, wear funny hats, and dance and cavort with beggars.

Whatever the minister's mien in public, it is vital that time be spent for private fun, lunacy, and restoration; for climbing a mountain or going to the seaside; for dreaming dreams and writing poetry and riding Ferris wheels; for letting the warm juices of childhood flow again in aging veins.

"All work and no play makes Jack a dull boy" is true for those in ministry. Those who don't regularly refresh themselves by taking time off from their duties work themselves into an unreal sense of what life is like and how it ought to be lived. They become too serious about their own philosophies and theologies, and forget how to laugh at their own pomposities. Their sermons become stupid and pedantic, and their prayers fatuous and hollow.

Only a person engaged with life at every level, from the sublime to the ridiculous, is worthy of representing the gospel of Christ.

13

Ask yourself frequently, *What kind of diet are my people getting?*

We cluck our tongues at mothers in the check-out line at the super-market whose baskets are full of high-calorie, low-nutrition snack foods and soda pop. But are we as guilty as they are when it comes to what we feed our congregations? Do we let our people gorge on religious fluff-and-stuff when they ought to be doing hard thinking about their spirituality and how it relates to their work in the modern world?

Many churches are proud of being like snack counters, where their members can find slickly packaged sweet stuffs that will produce a momentary high but are definitely unhealthy in the long run. They give them snappy little choruses, flaky, easy-to-swallow homilies, and fellowship gatherings full of pep-rally slogans but short on substantive challenges to the status quo.

These things work, they insist—just look at the attendance figures! Of course they do, if that's all you're aiming for.

But the kingdom of God is about something a lot deeper and more confrontational than that. It's about inner growth and expansion of the spirit, not membership growth and expansion of the parking lot. It's about *equipping* the saints, not *entertaining* them.

So sit down in a quiet place for a few minutes and take an inventory of what you're providing in your church's overall diet for its members. What does the average member, of whatever age, consume from your "cafeteria" in a month or a year? Is it healthy and constructive? Does it build strong Christians with a spirit of enterprise and devotion?

If it doesn't . . . . Well, you're the dietician at your church. You're the one who has to begin addressing the problem.

Talk real sense in your sermons, prayers, and pastoral communications, not holy twaddle.

Amy Dickinson, the "new Ann Landers" in the *Chicago Tribune*'s syndicated "Ask Amy" column, says she knows there's somebody out there among her readers with a "horses**t" stamp waiting to use it on whatever she has written. So she's very careful to keep her answers to people's questions real and sensible as well as entertaining.

We pastors may not think so, but there are a lot of people in our parishes who are waiting to do the same thing to our public pronouncements. It is easy, when we have a platform of the kind we have, to make silly or even preposterous statements, and every one we make weakens the strength of our witness and the effectiveness of our ministry.

The story is told of an English king who was listening to a sermon when he tamped the floor with his mace and said to the preacher, "Either talk sense or come down!"

"No, sir," the preacher answered. "As God is my witness, I will not!"

We are under an obligation to talk sense to our people and to speak to them in real time about real things, so that their lives are transformed and they can cope effectively with the stress and strain of daily existence. Being ministers doesn't give us carte blanche to deliver meaningless pronouncements; on the contrary, it puts us under the obligation to speak the truth in love and to do it as sanely and persuasively as possible.

As the Apostle Paul put it in his second letter to the Corinthians, we should behave in the world "with frankness and godly sincerity" (2 Cor 1:12).

15

Learn to put your faith—and the historic Christian faith—into stories.

Who doesn't love a good story? Even nervous, wriggling little children are captivated by well-told narratives. Much of what we know about the Judeo-Christian faith comes to us by way of stories. And much of what we remember about sermons we've heard is the stories they employed.

There has never been a great preacher who has not been a master storyteller. Henry Ward Beecher, Charles Haddon Spurgeon, F. W. Robertson, Thomas Chalmers, Dwight L. Moody, Phillips Brooks, Henry Drummond, Alexander Whyte, Paul Scherer, Harry Emerson Fosdick, George A. Buttrick, Ralph Sockman, W. R. Inge, Helmut Thielicke, and James Stewart were all gifted tale spinners.

It stands to reason that a faith whose center is the incarnation is best proclaimed through the stories that are the incarnation of the message.

All the names I listed above were those of male preachers, but when I was teaching preaching at Vanderbilt Divinity School a few years ago, I learned that women are wonderful storytellers too, and often have a greater sense of how the gospel becomes incarnate in daily life than men do.

If you are not a good storyteller, you can become a better one than you are. Find and read a copy of W. E. Sangster's *The Craft of Sermon Illustration* (Baker Books, 1973). Read and ingest the sermons of great narrative preachers, like the ones above. Take a class in storytelling. Attend one of the national storytelling conventions, such as the one held in Johnson City, Tennessee, each year. Begin to note how your congregation perks up when you get into a story that intrigues them.[1] Attempt to preach using sermons that are extended stories. Try preaching to your adult congregation the kind of illustrative sermon you would use for a children's sermon. Think *story* instead of argument or declamation.

If Jesus used parables as a vehicle for explaining the kingdom, how can we hope to do better?

Note

1. Again, a breach of modesty, but Chalice Press recently published my own *Stories that Shaped My Life and Ministry* (2011).

16

Make the keeping of a preacher's notebook one of your top priorities.

Once, when I was teaching homiletics, Dr. Ernest Campbell, the minister of Riverside Church in New York, was a guest in one of my classes. He didn't lecture. He merely opened the floor to questions. The first question someone asked was, "Dr. Campbell, how do you come up with a top-flight sermon every Sunday?"

Campbell didn't bat an eye. He reached into his coat pocket, removed a small black notebook, and laid it on the table in front of him. "I'd be lost without this," he said. "I carry it everywhere, and enter into it every sermon idea, every clever phrase, and every illustration I come across. I must have about thirty of these notebooks now. And every once in a while, I just sit down for an hour or two and go through them, gleaning the thoughts that are ripening there for my use."

I was delighted, because I had been insisting for years that students develop this habit while still in seminary. Since then, I have had several say to me, either in person or by mail, that it was the best habit they ever developed as preachers and they would be eternally grateful for my having introduced them to it.

Not long ago, one of my former students, who is now pastor of a church in Little Rock, sent me a packet in the mail. When I opened it, it contained a fine, well-made pocket notebook made by the Moleskine Company, and a letter thanking me for having made the preacher's notebook a part of his distinguished life and career. That notebook is now half full of stories and quotations I have been collecting since receiving it.

One little story is about a British crime drama on television, which involved the theft of a $15-million red diamond in the rough and the possibility that some jeweler would be asked to cut it. One of the policemen on the case remarked, "Whoever cuts that stone, it will change his life!"

And there is a quotation from an e-mail message I received: "We need to stop telling God how big our storms are and start telling our storms how big God is!"

As I always told my students, if you don't get these things down when they come to you, you will forget them and never be able to recover them. But once ensconced in a notebook, they will never get away from you. You can feed out of those notebooks for decades to come.

17

Attend to your soul.

That may sound like a fatuous remark when made to a minister, but it isn't. Many ministers forget to look after their souls once they get into their life's work, assuming their inner lives will take care of themselves. Unfortunately, they don't. They're a lot like our bodies, which grow fat and diseased when we don't watch our intake of food and get our quota of exercise.

I recently heard from a minister who neglected his soul. He had founded his own congregation and it had become a flourishing church. In the meantime, he failed to look after himself. Although he was married and had delightful children, he let his appetites begin to stray. Before long, he became embroiled in several relationships with women on the Internet and began to have secret meetings with them. In a matter of only a few weeks, he had destroyed his entire ministry and wrecked his family life.

My son Eric is a minister who became a Jungian psychologist. Deciding to write his PhD thesis on ministers who stopped being clergy, he met and interviewed a number of people who testified that they had lost their souls in the church. Almost without exception, they said they were able to manage their souls better outside the ministry than inside it. It is a frightening prospect!

How does one attend to his or her soul?

By taking time, to begin with. By reflecting, questioning the self, dreaming about life's big themes, being with people whose minds are calm and deep and stimulating. Sometimes by having psychoanalysis or practicing meditation. By developing an inner exercise routine that trains the fiber of the soul the way running or swimming or doing aerobics trains the muscles of the body.

Jesus said, "If salt has lost its taste, how can its saltiness be restored? It is no longer good for anything, but is thrown out and trampled under foot" (Matt 5:13).

That's a real judgment on ministers, isn't it? If we've lost touch with our own souls, how can we put others in touch with theirs?

18

Be wise as serpents and innocent as doves.

This was Jesus' saying, of course, when he sent out his disciples (Matt 10:16). But it still applies to his servants today.

Being engaged by the work of the church, we hate to think that we're going out among wolves, as Jesus' saying predicted, but the truth is, we are. Billy Sunday is credited with saying that not everyone who goes to church is a Christian, any more than somebody entering a garage becomes a car. So there are some pretty mean people in most churches, even if most are good and kind.

I mention this only to remind you not to take it personally when some of the folks in your church give you a hard time, as they will. It isn't you they have a quarrel with; it's the office of the minister or the leadership of the church. They might be even worse toward somebody else.

Try to stay focused on your job and not let these people deflect you from it. That's what God expects of you.

I once heard Carlyle Marney, a great Baptist minister who pastored churches in Texas and North Carolina, tell about a faithful old dog somebody owned in his hometown of Harriman, Tennessee. The dog was so trustworthy that its owners would send it down to the local butcher's shop to fetch the meat they had ordered. On the way home, all the mutts along the way would fall in beside him, barking and pulling at his ears to get him to release the package. But he simply ignored them, Marney related, and continued on his way as if nothing were happening.

That's the way it is for good ministers. They don't turn aside from their work just because other people pester them along the way. As Marney said, they just bring the bacon home.

I'm not sure about being innocent as doves. I think what Jesus meant was that we're to be as pure as doves, even though part of us is learning to be as wise as a serpent. Our fellowship with Christ is supposed to keep us kind and gentle while others take potshots at us from every side.

One of the highest compliments I ever had from a parishioner came from Hollywood attorney Thomas Hunter Russell, who spoke at my birthday party the year I turned seventy. Tom had sometimes been one of my severest critics when I was minister of his church in Los Angeles, and there were times when I thought he'd like to strangle me. But at my party, he called me "Gentleman John," because I had never spoken harshly to him when he was berating me. It was a great tribute, and one I'll always treasure.

I hope it fell under the category of being "innocent as a dove."

19

Keep a journal.

It doesn't have to be fancy or literary or anything like that. But keep a daily record of your thoughts and your work as you go about your tasks in ministry. Someday you'll be glad you did.

Keeping a journal does three things:

First, it forces you to be reflective about your days, so that no day goes by without your thinking about what happened in its course.

Second, it provides you with an important record of names and events you'll someday be glad you have when trying to remember a particular person or verify some forgotten turn of events.

Third, it will permit you to look back across your ministry and notice themes and patterns in the way it progressed, in what you were thinking, and in what your spiritual life was like.

Also, if you ever feel called upon to write your autobiography, you will have a day-by-day record that will be far superior to anything you try to recollect on your own. As Mark Twain once said, he had such a good memory that he could even remember things that never happened. Years after an event, we need accurate records; otherwise, we are liable to become as fanciful as some of the ancient historians.

You might want to check out a few great diarists to see how they treated the material of their daily lives. What they wrote ranged from the trivial (Samuel Pepys and James Boswell) to the philosophical and profound (Søren Kierkegaard and Albert Camus). You will find your own style and manner. The important thing is to write things down so you can review and meditate on them.

Oh, and one more thing. Try to write legibly. Sometimes my own scrawl has become almost unreadable after an interval of a few years. I have known one or two ministers who use their computers for this reason, jotting down a few paragraphs each night before going to bed. Suit yourself. But you will be grateful, years from now, for legibility.

20

Read the Bible as if you were listening to it, not as if you had written it.

I forget about whom this was once said, but someone remarked that a great Scottish preacher always read the Bible publicly this way—as if he were listening, not dictating—and that person thought it was wonderful. I agree. But it goes for your reading Scripture in private as well as when you read it from the lectern.

Sometimes I think we become too familiar with the Bible and treat it too casually, as if we ourselves had written it. Even Billy Graham, who used to hold up a flexible Bible (so that it fell gracefully over his hand, as if it were the wings of a bird) and quote it in a stentorian, rhetorical voice, may have been guilty of this.

I believe as much as the next person in really studying the Scriptures, and slicing and dicing them until they give up their meaning in lambent moments of inspiration. But sometimes I also like to remember the reverence with which I held the Bible when I was a youngster and wouldn't even make a mark on its pages because it was so sacred to me.

There was once a bibliophile who loved books so much that when he received a packet of books from his bookseller in Edinburgh or London, he would hold them upside down while cutting the pages (in a time when pages weren't uniformly separated before books were sold) lest he lose some of their wonderful spirit before he was ready to read them.

I'd like to feel this way about the Bible at least part of the time, and imagine its very antiquity as I approach it. I'd like to think I will hear a voice in its pages that transcends all time and space to speak the very word I need to hear—and my people after me, of course. Somehow, I believe I hear more this way than I do when I'm too casual or cavalier in my approach to it.

21

Treat your present church as if it were your last.

Too many ministers use churches as stepping-stones to other churches. Even in episcopal systems, they think, *If I do a good job here and some-body notices, I will move on to something bigger!*

Remember, there are no little, inconsequential churches in the kingdom of God. Every one is an arena of the Holy Spirit, a place of potential joy and excitement.

I received an e-mail the other day from a former student who is now the pastor of a church in rural Nebraska. He told me proudly about all the things his people are doing—delivering meals to shut-ins, providing housing for the poor, offering counseling services to those who need it, and praying for almost everything and everybody they can think of. His is a poor church. They are meeting this winter in the church basement to save money by not heating their big sanctuary.

Inconsequential? Not by God's standards. I know a lot of grandiose churches in New York, Chicago, and Los Angeles that should wish to be as big in God's eyes!

So enjoy your people where you are and give your ministry in their midst your very best. Don't be preaching sermons and making con-tacts and writing the books that you think will get you someplace else. Concentrate on being the best pastor, the best counselor, the best preacher, and the best CEO you can be right where you are.

If God chooses to give you a larger responsibility some day, that might be a mixed blessing. I've never known a minister in a big church who didn't look back fondly to his or her days in a little one-room church in a small community, and sometimes wish to be back there!

22

Don't play the blame game.

Be man or woman enough to stand up and accept responsibility for anything that goes wrong.

There will be plenty of temptation to try to reassign blame to someone other than yourself, and to do it often. But you will respect yourself more, and your people will respect you more too, if you are bigger than that and simply, unequivocally say to your board or congregation, "I made a mistake and I'm sorry."

I once heard a speaker tell a ministers' gathering about a pastor who, when he left his church, placed a large envelope addressed to his successor in the center drawer of the big desk in his study. It contained a brief letter and three smaller envelopes. The letter instructed the successor to open a letter each time he or she felt that the world would come to an end if it weren't opened.

For a year or so, the new minister forgot about the envelopes because everything went well. He was in what we all know as the "honeymoon" phase of his ministry. But then the waters got a little rough. The minister made a few mistakes, and people were shifting uneasily, thinking perhaps they had a lemon. Recalling the envelopes, the minister took out the first one and opened it.

It said, "Blame the former pastor."

"Ah," thought the minister, "I can do that. I've just been given permission." So he began laying all the blame for mistakes he'd made on the last minister.

Miraculously, it seemed to calm the waters almost at once.

A year or so later, the minister hit another bad patch and was drawing a lot of criticism. Experts say there is often a kind of uprising after the second anniversary of a minister's pastorate, and this was it. So the minister went back to the cache of envelopes and opened the second.

It said, "Blame the denomination."

"Aha," said the minister to himself, "that's a very good idea. A lot of our people aren't comfortable with some of the denomination's actions in recent months. I'll do it."

Again, the waters grew miraculously calm, almost as if the Lord himself had instructed them to stop roiling so much.

Now everything went smoothly for three more years—until the fifth year of the minister's pastorate, which for some unknown reason is almost always a difficult time. Then it seemed that all hell broke loose in almost every area within the parish. Desperately, the minister withdrew the third and final letter from the desk drawer and opened it with trembling hands.

It said, "Prepare three envelopes."

The ministers who listened to this story guffawed at its punch line. But I wondered if there wasn't almost too much merriment, as if most of them had been down to their third letter a time or two and knew what it was all about.

A truly good minister never tries to reassign blame from him- or herself, but stands courageously before the congregation and says, "If you want to blame someone for what has happened—for the drop in attendance, the lag in pledges, the staff problems, the trouble in the youth group, the increasing shabbiness of the building—blame me. God has given me big shoulders, and I will be your scapegoat. Now I'm going to ask you to forgive me, and let's all work together to make things function as they should!"

The people who matter most in your congregation will forgive you and put their shoulders to the wheel.

23

"The music department is the war department of the church."

Those aren't my words. They have been around longer than I have, maybe ever since Johann Sebastian Bach's pastor complained that the organ was too loud. And truer words were never spoken.

I don't mean that you shouldn't ever try to get the congregation to sing some new hymns or ask the choir to stop using so many Latin anthems or suggest to the organist that he may be playing a tad loud for some of the old folks whose hearing aids give them fits on the high notes. I only mean that you have to be very, very careful when you do it—sort of like tiptoeing through a pit of sleeping vipers without waking them.

Dealing with the music situation was the very first problem I encountered in my very first parish. It was a small country church and there was only one young woman in the community who could play the piano at all, even poorly. She had recently married and moved away. Her mother, who enjoyed the visibility her daughter's playing had provided, sat on the piano bench every Sunday as if to defy anyone who might have designs on taking her daughter's place. Everybody was baffled about what to do.

Fortunately for me, the problem simply dissolved. Overhearing a lot of the gossip about her bizarre behavior, the mother got mad at the church and transferred to another church several miles away. I was saved from certain catastrophe without having to deal with it at all.

Years later, the chair of my church's music committee—in a much larger church this time—came to me with anguish in her voice to say that we simply had to ask the minister of music to leave because he had grown too old to do his job properly and was allowing the children's choir and youth choir to flounder so he could devote all his attention to the adult choir. I listened to all the embellishments on her complaint, and, assured that what she was telling me was the unanimous opinion of the committee, took the minister of music to lunch to talk about it.

The lunch went quite well. In fact, the minister of music brought up the subject of his retirement so I didn't have to address it at all. I helped him—perhaps a bit too cheerfully—to think about when he'd like to schedule his leaving and how we should go about finding a replacement.

I thought it had all gone extremely well.

Then his wife got wind of what was happening and the detritus hit the fan.

I had never seen anything as near to the Third World War blow up so quickly. Within two days, everybody in the community was talking about how the pastor had given the minister of music an ultimatum to get out and how unfair it was to treat a man of his age so disrespectfully. Even the members of the music committee were angry with me, and for weeks several choir members glared at me ferociously as they processed down the aisle each Sunday during the opening hymn.

The outcome, though, wasn't as disastrous as I thought it might be. Eventually something else diverted everybody's attention, and a competent music committee interviewed and eventually called a new minister of music.

But even years later, I still feel bad about how what had seemed such an amicable settlement to a matter I didn't initiate blew up on me in the process and left some bitterness in the hearts of a lot of people who never understood what had really happened.

So, even though the saying "The music department is the war department of the church" isn't mine, I endorse it whole-heartedly. In the words of the old sergeant on *NYPD Blue*, "Be careful out there!"

24

Always keep a confidence—even if you're being tortured to reveal it.

Nothing sinks a counseling ministry, or even pastoral friendships, faster than a loose tongue about something someone has confided to you, even if it was only in the hall or in the greeting line after church on Sunday.

It might be a good idea if every pastor kept on his or her desk a statue of those three little monkeys who have their paws in different locations to mime "See no evil, hear no evil, speak no evil." We all see and hear plenty of evil, there's no doubt about that. We're in the wrong business not to. But we'd better be plenty careful about not speaking any evil—or at least not repeating anything we've heard from parishioners about themselves and the people they know.

It's tempting to tell juicy tidbits we know. There's always someone eager to hear them. It can even give us a feeling of camaraderie with the person we're spreading the word to. And sometimes we almost feel as if it's our duty, especially if what we're sharing affects the person we're talking to.

But consider this: every time you tell something confidential to someone else, won't that person inevitably think, *If my pastor is telling this kind of information to me about so-and-so, what will he or she do with the information I entrust?*

It isn't easy to muzzle the tongue. Most people prefer a nice, juicy bit of gossip to a cold beer or a rubdown. But it is absolutely essential for ministers to learn to control what passes through their mouths.

Remember what the book of James says about the tongue: that it is like the rudder of a great ship, with the power to determine its direction, and that it is also like a torch that is able to set a whole forest ablaze! Not only that: it says the original fire that lights the tongue is the fire of hell itself (James 3:1-6)!

So be careful about MM—mouth management—and tell something on yourself if you really feel compelled to share some personal or confidential information.

25

Rise above your seminary education as quickly as you can.

I know that sounds silly. After all, you went to seminary in order to become a minister. You admired a lot of your professors for what they knew. You are proud to have learned a lot and to have graduated from the program.

Why on earth should you want to forget that you went to seminary?

For the same reason lawyers have to get over how impressed they were with going to law school and doctors have to get over how impressed they were with going to medical school. Because what one learns in a professional school of any kind is only the beginning, only the very minimal rudiments of what a person needs in order to relate to people in the greater world and serve them as a mature professional.

Dora Saint, the English novelist who wrote under the pseudonym Miss Read, described in *Life in Fairacre* a young school teacher named Hilary Jackson who was so impressed by a psychology teacher she had in graduate school named Miss Crabbe that she was forever boring other people by referring to Miss Crabbe's rather idiosyncratic theories about education. It wasn't that what she said was wrong, only that it was usually inconsequential and bereft of meaningful context. Hilary sounded like a pompous twit for not having simply run Miss Crabbe's philosophy and ideas through the sieve of her own personality to match them to the situation she presently faced.

In the same way, it is a mark of immaturity for a minister to needlessly toss around the names and theories of various theologians, ethicists, and biblical scholars. Instead of piquing people's curiosity about their subjects and ideas, it only marks the minister as an impressionable beginner who hasn't yet digested all the bits of material dished out in seminary.

What did Mark Twain say when his wife tried to cure him of swearing by memorizing a string of oaths and expressing them one day in his presence? "You have heard the words, my dear, but you will never master the tune."

When ministers learn the tune, they don't brandish names and ideas with the same alacrity; instead, they talk the comfortable, more natural lingo of the home folks.

26

Always be yourself, not a parson.

I know you're an ordained minister and you have to act the part in order to convince yourself that it's true. But try not to be any more ministerial than absolutely necessary, even if being ministerial means getting a 10 percent discount at a local grocery store.

Paul said "we have this treasure [the gospel] in earthen vessels" (2 Cor 4:7), so it's better if we don't try to be Ming vases or cloisonné decanters, for it is more important to remind people that God becomes incarnate in people like them than to suggest that God dwells in people with unnaturally deep voices, a self-righteous bearing, and a tendency toward primness and egotism.

It will be tempting, when people fawn over you because you're a minister, to embody their ideals in a false manner and pious demeanor, fulfilling their expectations. But remember that when you do this you are forswearing your natural self, which is able to give individuality and distinctiveness to your special calling.

Don't go to the other extreme, of having to demonstrate to all and sundry that you are a regular person by salting your language with profanity, drinking too much wine or beer, and wanting to talk ball games when everybody else is hoping to tap your understanding of faith and spirituality. I have known ministers who reveled in shocking their parishioners with displays of worldliness or impressing them with a kind of stiff-necked urbanity. What they actually succeeded in doing was making a mockery of their ordination by being someone other than the person who was ordained.

I forget who it was who talked about "certain ingrained clerical peculiarities," but I think it was George Eliot who said that when she

tried to think of Christ, she had to shut her eyes lest she behold a
parson. The point is, the pastor as a fake and a fraud has had a long
history in the world's literature and experience, and it is always far
better for the new minister to learn from the outset to be him- or herself and not join that long line of imitation clerics the world expects us
to be.

27

Be punctual.

Not to a fault, so that your punctuality appears to be a mere obsession, but in general, so people know you to be a responsible human being who is mindful of the needs and schedules of others.

It's true that heaven doesn't run on a railroad timetable, and that making a point of being on time for meetings and engagements can seem excessively Pecksniffian. But having a decent regard for timeliness (i.e., punctuality) is the mark of a thoughtful personality, which is part of what we hope every converted and baptized Christian aims for.

It simply doesn't look right—and isn't right—for ministers to be cavalier about showing up on time for an engagement as if they couldn't be bothered to conform to normal expectations because they are special people whose privileged status was confirmed by an ordaining council.

I used to see them in seminary—students who couldn't get to class on time and didn't have the work prepared when they came or else didn't come at all when it suited them to be elsewhere. "Dear God," I would think, "teach them some manners before they get to a parish and pull this kind of irresponsible behavior on their congregants, or they'll spend the rest of their lives missing half of what's going on and then being late for their own funerals."

And then, years later, I would see them on my own staff—young men and women as undisciplined as a rag mop, rushing in late to meetings and having forgotten to do their assignments for the group, or flying down the hall on Sunday morning, bumping into parishioners as they went, because they were late showing up for a class or an important meeting.

I'm not sure about heaven, but Dante must have had a special place in hell reserved for people who could never observe the common decency of being on time for appointments—maybe a room on the far end of nowhere that they are still trying to locate after everybody else has settled in.

28

Keep a healthy theological curiosity as long as you live.

I know you were supposed to be well-educated about the way everything works by the time you left seminary, but if you were anything like me, you hadn't even begun to understand how theology really works.

Frederick Buechner had the right idea when he said in *The Alphabet of Grace* (HarperOne, 1989), "At its heart, most theology, like most fiction, is essentially autobiography. Aquinas, Calvin, Barth, Tillich, working out their systems in their own ways and in their own language, are all telling us the stories of their lives, and if you press them far enough, even at their most cerebral and forbidding, you find an experience of flesh and blood, a human face smiling or frowning or weeping or covering its eyes before something that happened once." Amen to that!

You can't be an honest and effective minister for very long without becoming a serious theologian. Whenever you bury a precious little child or take a battered wife to a shelter or sit by the bed of an ailing spouse or hold the hand of a businessperson who has just lost everything, you will be working on another chapter in your own theology. Not the one you learned in seminary, but the one being developed in your own mind and heart as you deal with the hard questions of life.

Maybe you didn't bargain to be a theologian when you accepted your call to the ministry, but that doesn't matter. It was in the small print, and there is no way you can avoid it unless you are a callous impostor or an unforgivable shirker of your duty. People want answers. They *need* answers. And the only way you'll have answers to share—satisfactory ones, at least—is if you continue to wrestle with important matters all of your ministry and can give them your latest take on what is the unforgivable sin or who we're going to meet in heaven when we get there.

What I'm saying has particular relevance today, when the electronic revolution has produced a fierce kind of globalism that is chewing up and spitting out all the old theological understandings. We have to rethink everything from the bottom up and inside out before we can preach a single sermon, baptize a single child, or pray over a single casket.

Read the new theologians. Go back and read the old ones. Pray for a strong digestion so you can take in all that the big minds are saying. And then dare to come to a few vital conclusions for yourself that square with your current understanding of life and the world.

If you don't, you're AWOL—agnostic without license.

29

Preach the occasional series of sermons.

Church members often like the connectedness of a few sermons in a row, especially if they are informative and interesting.

For the minister, there are several advantages to preaching series.

First, the study and reflection that go into the subject matter are more economical, for they apply to the entire series and not to a single sermon. If you are preaching on the great "I Am" passages in John, for example—Jesus as the Way, the Good Shepherd, the Light of the World, and so on—the biblical research you should do to inform a single sermon can be spread over a number of sermons.

Second, there is a cumulative effect to several sermons preached in a row. The second sermon in the series draws on the first, and the third on both the first and the second, and so on. People's anticipation also grows cumulatively.

Third, key ideas and concepts are reinforced by being referenced again and again, and not left behind after a single sermon, so there is an educational advantage not to be derived from individual sermons.

And fourth, the planning of a series is often easier than the planning of a single sermon, because the preacher has more space in which to deal with significant ideas and can work out his or her thoughts on a broader canvas.

How long should the ideal series be? Long enough to link ideas and images together from Sunday to Sunday without becoming boring or predictable. Most preachers find that the ideal number is from three to six, although a particularly interesting series, say, on the Ten Commandments or the Twelve Apostles, might easily run longer.

I sometimes preached what I called a *homileticus interruptus,* giving three or four sermons in a row, pausing for a Sunday or two while I preached on other things, then returning to the series for a few more Sundays.

Perhaps the most important thing to remember is that the entire series must be vibrant and interesting, filled with solid information and memorable illustrations. Otherwise, people will count the Sundays until the minister gets off the present series and dread the time when another is commenced.

30

Wear appropriate dress for every occasion, especially at work or in the pulpit.

Rebellious pastors sometimes refuse to wear ties—or stockings, in the case of women ministers—in the office or behind the pulpit, claiming that it sets them apart from the majority of church members who dress more casually. Even some big-name television preachers like to appear in open-necked shirts or casual skirts and blouses.

This is a pretty sticky issue today, when workplaces often dress down on certain days of the week. Personally, I agree with the traditionalists on this one, and believe that the minister ought to dress "up" for public occasions, even if they dress down at other times.

Think about people in other professional lines of work. How do you feel when you go into a bank where everybody is dressed casually, even to the point of slovenliness? Or into an attorney's office, where the lawyer looks as if she just came in from the tennis court or golf links?

I confess that it bothers me to visit a physician who doesn't wear a tie, or, if it's a woman, stockings and a neat pair of shoes. I'm not sure why that is, unless it has to do with professional courtesy and the sense that this person thinks I'm important enough to meet me in at least a professional outfit.

There are still a lot of church members—admittedly most of them older, more traditional folks—who like to see their ministers in suits or robes on Sunday morning, and wearing shoes that match the robes.

One minister told me that he was chided on his first Sunday in a new parish because he wore brown shoes with a black suit. So from then on, he wore black shoes on Sunday. Until his last Sunday. On his final Sunday as the pastor of that church, he came down the aisle behind the choir wearing a pair of white tennis shoes! It was his way of saying, "I obeyed the rules while I was your pastor, but now that I'm leaving, I'm reclaiming my personal freedom to wear whatever I like."

It may seem to be a small thing. It probably is. But remember the maxim "Pick your battles." Don't engage people's disapproval on such a minor thing as what you wear. Meet their expectations and everybody—including you—will be happy.

31

Be faithful about answering notes, letters, e-mails, and phone calls.

This is a matter of common courtesy. It shows people that you care and are responsible. Think of it this way: they'll be happier to have you marry their children and bury their dead if they know you are a disciplined, responsive person.

We appear to live in a society today in which few people exhibit this kind of discipline. Few people remember to call back when we leave a message, and many don't answer our letters or e-mails. It's as if most of the world is disconnected and the lines that once joined us together lie like a plateful of spaghetti with the ends all pointing in different directions.

If you are faithful about answering people when they've attempted to contact you, you impose a little order within their otherwise chaotic existence. They come to identify the faith you represent with the sense of order that makes their lives more comfortable. So when you are a disciplined responder, you are somehow preaching the gospel of peace and love.

Promptness in answering is also an important part of the formula.

When I went to a certain church to help an older minister preparing for retirement, I found its communication system in unbelievable disarray. The minister's secretary was often discouraging to people who tried to contact him, thinking she was doing him a favor. Even when she permitted calls, letters, and e-mails to get through, he usually didn't answer them, or if he did, he sometimes took weeks to do it.

As people learned that I was prompt to answer any form of communication, I became deluged with calls and e-mails. When I returned them within a few hours, people expressed amazement that they had found any kind of resonance among the ministers. It seemed to revive their sense of faith in the pastorate.

Of course it takes time and effort to communicate faithfully. But what are we in the ministry for, if not to serve the people of God?

32

Be kind and attentive to everybody—literally everybody—on your staff, including the cooks and janitors, if you have them.

It was always my thesis that the church staff should model the very idea of church to the congregation—that by living harmoniously with one another, handling problems in a civil and orderly manner, and coming to one another's aid whenever there was a personal need of any kind, we preached an effective sermon to our whole congregation about how they themselves were to live in the greater world.

But this only works if the pastor is a loving, caring individual who exudes a spirit of warmth and fellowship to everybody on the staff, from the volunteers and part-time staff to the secretaries and other ministers.

It isn't hard. Think father—or, in the case of a female minister, mother—and how a good father or mother operates at the center of a family, seeing that everyone has what is needed, including love and attention. I like the way Catholics and Episcopalians call their priests "Father." I'm not sure what Episcopalians call female priests. Is it "Mother"? It should be. In either case, the senior minister is like a solicitous parent who is there for everybody else.

To be realistic, there will be bad apples among the staff personnel, just as there are bad apples in almost every family. Some will sow discord with the others and seem to be more trouble than they're worth. I once heard a prominent minister say that his ministry would be easy if only he didn't have a staff to deal with. "They take more of my time," he confessed, "than the congregation."

But what thoughtful, intentional parent rejects a child because the child is unruly or a troublemaker? Instead, the parent spends more time with that child and works harder to try to make him or her feel welcome and important in the midst of a busy family.

In all my years as a parish minister, I can remember only two staff members who were so devious and disruptive that I wanted to be rid of them for the sake of the other staff members. As it turned out, I left before either of them did, and while we were together, I truly believe that neither could honestly say I didn't treat them as fairly and kindly as I treated any other member of the team.

Looking back, I'm glad I didn't terminate either of them, even though they deserved termination. The principle of the family relationship proved stronger than my need to resolve a festering problem.

33

Make your sermons available in printed form for people to take and reread or pass them on to others.

Preferably, have them out on a table to be picked up on the day they are preached—after the service, of course, as you wouldn't want to see people in the congregation following the printed sermons and checking to see if you made mistakes delivering them. At least have them on display by the next Sunday, while the sermons are still reasonably fresh in people's minds.

Assuming that you write your sermons out (and I hope you do, for it is the best way to grow as a homiletician), it is easy enough to produce printed versions straight from the computer and your own simple printer.

In larger churches with media expertise, CDs or DVDs supplement the printed sermons and are available immediately after a service, while the printed sermons themselves are produced in more lavish editions, with stylish covers. But it is perfectly all right in smaller churches merely to run off the sermons on regular copy paper, staple them in the corner, and set them out that way.

You may be amazed at the extended half-life a published sermon can have. I have had people twenty or thirty years after I preached a particular sermon tell me that they still have the sermon and often read it for one reason or another. Several people have said they have a whole collection of my sermons and enjoy taking them out and going through them for an extended period of time, especially after they have had a death in the family or some other crisis that has brought them to a new place of thoughtfulness and contemplation.

One fine minister I know told me that a minister's printed sermon literally changed his life. He was in the US Navy and stationed in Hawaii. He had been dating a girl there for some time. One day she told him she was tired of the relationship and wanted to break off with him. He went to his bunk and cried and felt terribly despondent.

Then he remembered that someone had sent him a sermon from a New York church whose title appealed to his sense of loss. He dug through his papers, found the sermon, and read it. It gave him new hope and turned his life around.

A few years later, when he became an actor and moved to New York, this man went to the minister whose sermon he had read and told him how important it had been to him. In an acting class, he mentioned this to a young woman, and she told him she belonged to the church where that minister was the pastor. They started going to church together and eventually fell in love and got married. They had a little girl and began taking her to Sunday school

When the church needed a new minister of education, he and his wife went to the minister and said they'd like to try filling the position until a permanent leader was found. They did such a terrific job that they occupied the post for seven years. During that time the man felt called to the ministry and went to seminary.

Now he is the minister of a church in upstate New York, and he and his wife have become pillars of their community. And it all began—his whole religious pilgrimage—from his reading a printed sermon that someone thought was good enough to send him while he was in the military.

34

Develop friendships with other ministers in your community, if you can, and treasure what these relation- ships can mean to your congregation as well as to you.

I have always found ministers to be among the most special people I've known. Their thoughts, their jokes, their special knowledge about doing things, and especially their warm friendships have blessed my life beyond telling.

Oh, I know some of them can be stuffy or pretentious, standoffish or carping—all very human qualities. But most of them are among the choicest people I've had the privilege of knowing. They have lifted me, expanded my horizons, and enlarged my sense of who God is and how God relates to the world. Now, at a time when I no longer have a congregation, I keep up with many of them by phone and e-mail. There isn't a day that passes when I don't hear from two or three of them, and I always feel recharged when we have had a little visit.

Be on the lookout, especially for a minister who can be your pastor when you need one. Every pastor needs a pastor as much as his or her parishioners do. So go out and find one who fits the bill for you. And while you're at it, look for ones for whom you can be a pastor.

If your community doesn't have a ministerial association, think about starting one. Just send out a communiqué to all the pastors in your area stating a date, time, and place, and use the first gathering to talk about what kind of organization you'd like to have.

What will all this mean to your congregation? For one thing, it will keep their pastor healthy. And for another, it will open and maintain communication among the churches, which is important for their sustained awareness, wisdom, and collective work in the community. I'll miss my bet if it doesn't lead to a lot of cooperative ventures and a generally higher level of Christian love and care for everybody.

35

Work the edges of your congregation and the middle will take care of itself.

Well, not entirely, but you get the picture. Many of your parishioners are "meeters and greeters" who naturally move toward the center of any organization. They'll be healthy and happy because they are in the midst of whatever is going on.

The people you have to worry about are the quieter, more private individuals who inhabit the outer bands of the congregation—the ones who don't always show up in church and usually go out a side entrance instead of coming through the line to shake hands with the pastor.

A minister friend in Oklahoma City once told me about the time he broke his habit of recessing with the choir and went to the narthex ahead of the benediction. When he did this, he saw a man sitting in a folding chair behind a row of artificial plants at the rear of the congregation, and, because he had never seen him before, he went over to the man and introduced himself.

"Oh, I know who you are," said the man. "I've been attending here for three or four years."

"I was astounded," said the pastor, "because I'd never seen the man in my life. It turned out he was a psychiatrist with a very private manner who didn't like to run into anybody when he came to church. He'd been sitting behind that row of plants for years and had never been involved with the church at all!"

Most of the peripheral folks aren't that self-effacing, but any minister with a little sensitivity knows who they are—older and middle-aged couples who aren't very sociable, busy young professionals who are eager to get to their phone calls when they leave church, shy teenagers who look at everything from the sidelines, people of all ages who feel like "rejects" or strangers even in the most familiar places.

I always made it a habit to keep an eye on these people and try to intercept their line of flight so I could meet and talk to them, learn who they were, and then follow up with a visit or phone chat during the week. This didn't always result in their moving to the middle of the congregation—in fact, that happened only occasionally—but I always felt better as a pastor to think I was keeping up with the sheep at the edge of the flock as well as those who naturally got my attention.

A few times, my giving these marginal folks some special attention actually resulted in their becoming more active and visible in the congregation, and I can recall at least two or three who really blossomed and moved into places of leadership.

36

"Jesus said 'Feed my sheep.' He didn't say 'Feed my giraffes.'"

This remark was made years ago by an old African-American minister from South Carolina who was speaking to one of our classes in the divinity school where I taught, and I have always thought it was one of the best pieces of advice our students ever received.

Some ministers don't need to hear it, but many, especially the brighter, more bookish ones, do.

It is a great temptation for a preacher to want to pitch the sermon in the highest key possible, so it sounds bright, intelligent, and well-crafted. But the effect of this is almost always disastrous. While it calls attention to the preacher's mind and educational level, it doesn't produce the kind of connectivity that is the *sine qua non* of all true communication.

Take the phrase "*sine qua non*" I just used. I wouldn't ever use that in a sermon unless I was caught on the spot and couldn't think of a better, plainer phrase in English. It means "without which, nothing." I'm not even sure it has a place in a book like this. I know it doesn't belong in a sermon.

Years ago, I chafed when I learned that the Sunday school publications for the denomination to which I belonged were all required to be at or below fourth-grade reading level—even the adult lessons. But over the decades I have seen the wisdom of that. Many adults in our congregations are functionally illiterate. Some of them aren't even comfortable reading a newspaper or listening to a TV news program.

Our challenge, then, is to couch the gospel in the most winsome, transparent language we can summon, and to do it so consistently that it becomes second nature to us and we wince if we ever hear a preacher doing otherwise. A good guide is to watch the faces of your parishioners as you preach. If they maintain eye contact with you and their faces are radiant with hope and understanding, then you are doing great. But if they ever begin to look puzzled and detached, you're in deep doo-doo.

I won't parse *that* phrase for you.

37

Minister to the wealthier, more prosperous people in your congregation as faithfully and eagerly as if they were poor.

I know that may sound silly, but think about it. It is human nature for us ministers to stand a little in awe of the wealthier folks in our congregations. After all, they see life from a vantage point most of us will never occupy. Money means power, and they have more power in the community (and even in the church) than other parishioners. And because we have so much respect for their position, we often neglect to be as concerned about their welfare as we are about the welfare of "ordinary" people.

It's true that wealthy people will often seek the help they feel they need. Yet sometimes they don't recognize their own neediness. Accustomed to ruling the world around them, they assume they can overcome personal difficulties on their own. However, it often turns out that they can't. Their usual strength for dealing with problems may not extend to their more intimate situations. They can be lonely, afraid, nervous, or afflicted by illness, just like everybody else; and when they are, they can be as lost and needy as anyone.

George Stewart was president of the First Colony Life Insurance Company in Lynchburg, Virginia, and I was his pastor. When First Colony was sold to Aetna Corporation, George remained as chairman of the board, went on Aetna's board as well, and received about $50 million as a bonus on the deal (about $200 million by today's standards). He was a tough negotiator and an iron-fisted CEO. But I remember sitting in George's office on several occasions when he would pour out his heart to me because he had no one else to talk to except his wife, whom he didn't want to burden with his problems.

He had run track in college. Now he weighed about 300 pounds and was worried about his heart. He had once had a simple, unquestioning faith. Now, after dealing with a lot of people, he was less certain of what he believed and whether there was an afterlife. In short, there were times when he needed a pastor he could talk with about the things that troubled him.

And George was only one of many. Like the man from Gerasa in the Gospels, his name was Legion.

Everybody needs pastoring—even the rich and powerful.

38

Think about having a lotto in your church.

Not to make money, though that might seem like a good idea to some. But to decide with whom the pastor ought to have lunch one day a week.

Most of us fall into patterns of eating with certain parishioners, usually board members or the most personable people in the congregation. But what about all the members who don't have this privilege or are too timid to seek it?

Imagine what it would be like to have a weekly or monthly lotto in which the name of a parishioner is drawn from a barrel of names (or a fishbowl, if yours is a small congregation) and is entitled to have lunch with you at a place of your choosing. Of course, it could prove embarrassing if some folks said they'd prefer not to have their names in the pot. But on the whole, wouldn't it be a clever way of putting you together on a regular basis with some people you'd probably otherwise never get to know?

I confess I never did this in any of my churches. I only thought about it recently. But I wish I had thought of it years ago. I can almost guarantee there are several good friendships across the years that I missed out on because we never ate together or had the kind of quality time that would have produced a lasting relationship.

I often pounced on a visitor or a church member and would say, "Let's have lunch next week!" and many of those occasions proved extremely rewarding. But a lotto would have presented this opportunity on a regular basis, and I can only imagine how much it might enhance the joy of one's pastorate.

39

Set an example for your people's giving by being a giver yourself.

"Ah," you say, "now you have stopped preaching and gone to meddling!" Sorry about that. But why shouldn't a minister give to the church just like everyone else? Don't the people deserve a pastor who considers him- or herself eligible for the same charge delivered to the congregation?

My wife and I agreed early in our marriage that we would tithe our income in the church to which we belonged. I never made a big deal out of tithing among the members, as I always thought spirituality leads to a kind of generosity not even touched by tithing. But I thought that our giving a tithe of the money that passed through our hands was the least of what we should be doing for the church I was trying to lead.

I didn't blow a trumpet about it. I can't recall that I ever announced that we were tithers. But I'm sure it got around. The people who counted the Sunday offerings and kept the books and sent out statements were bound to know, and, given the way people gossip about the pastor, I'm sure they passed on the word. I'm reasonably sure, too, that at least a few people became more faithful givers because they knew their pastor was giving.

I have known a few pastors who actually made a point of putting their pledge offerings into the plate on Sunday morning at the time when all the offerings were collected. They cued the ushers to pause long enough for one of them to extend a plate toward the pulpit, where they, quietly and without fanfare, laid an envelope into it. This was a little too obvious for my taste, but I have to admit it isn't a bad practice for those who are comfortable with it.

The same goes for special offerings during the church year—collections for a new Scout hut, reroofing the sanctuary, a jukebox for the youth group, a donation to hurricane victims, a wood fund for the poor. When the pastor puts his or her gift in first, it is a great encouragement to the rest of the congregation.

Model *prima pares unter*, the old Latin phrase about the leader of the church: "first among equals."

40

Always be generous about sharing praise and the limelight with staff members and parishioners.

If there's anything that kills the spirit of a congregation faster than having a minister who is a narcissist and doesn't like to share center stage with others, I don't know what it is. And if there's anything that engenders more joy in a congregation than a generous minister who is always saying a word of thanks to another staff member or person from the congregation, I don't know what that is either.

Generosity of this kind is contagious. When we praise a staff member for a job well done or an idea that was particularly helpful to the church, it not only encourages the staff member but also sets an example for the entire congregation about how to treat others. When we single out an individual or individuals in the congregation for commendation because they've done something wonderful or helpful, the same thing happens.

We can only imagine that there will be church members all over town sharing the same kind of warm spirit with people in their own homes, schools, and businesses because they witnessed it in church.

I know an older minister who exudes love and kindness toward his staff. There is rarely a Sunday when he doesn't single out someone on whom to bestow kudos for something accomplished in one of the departments of the church. His happiness acts as a virus for the entire church, and people always leave the service with a spring in their step or a smile on their faces.

Sometimes this pastor will have a gift to bestow from the pulpit for an act of kindness or generosity. Often, for the women, it is a box of candy or a bouquet of flowers. For the men, it is a book or a framed photograph. And the others in the congregation never seem jealous of those who have received such acknowledgment. They enjoy it as much as the recipients themselves.

41

Listen deeply to people's complaints and ferret out underlying reasons for their distress that may not be apparent on the surface.

Some ministers say they let people's unhappiness roll off of them like water off a duck's back. I understand what they mean: they don't want to let the harsh things people say to them affect their own sense of joy and well-being.

But people complain either because they have a legitimate gripe about something or because they're hurting and don't know how else to get the attention they want. Either way, it is important for us to listen to them with warm and attentive spirits.

If their complaints are legitimate—the temperature in the sanctuary is always too warm, the organist plays too loudly, the spaces in the parking lot are too small, the library lending time is too short, somebody needs to get the oak leaves out of the boxwoods along the church drive—then who better to see that things get done around the church than the minister? And if their complaints are only manifestations of some deeper cause in the person's life—say, a fretful loneliness or a loved one's illness—who better to deal with that than the minister?

I remember a woman in one of my parishes who was always coming to me about something she thought should be fixed. Most of the things were actually in need of redress, but after a while I began to suspect that she simply liked coming to talk to me, so I made a special effort to spend time with her and hear her life's story. She lived with an ailing husband who could no longer go out, so she spent much of her time confined to the home. I started going by to see her once a week. She would offer me tea and we would visit for a while. It wasn't long before she stopped complaining altogether. Instead, she would stop by on Sunday morning and say, with a smile on her face, "I look forward to seeing you this week."

In a sense, every complaint is an opportunity for the gospel!

42

See that the weekly worship service is always centered on God, not on having fellowship or pushing a program or the great sermon you're going to preach.

We too often forget to do this in the rush of the week's events and all the things we have to do.

Søren Kierkegaard understood. He said that we make the mistake of thinking that the congregation is sitting in the pews watching God and the minister make a show up front. What really happens is that God is in the pews and we are all putting on our act of adoration for the divine, not the other way around.

If you remember this every time you plan a worship service, it will subtly affect how you do it and the tone of the service that results. There will be a greater sense of holiness in the sanctuary, a real feeling that you and your people are coming before God to pay your respects and seek a divine blessing.

I have been in services where the minister seemed to think it was his job to say witty things and tell jokes and make all the people feel good, and where the music was the kind that people enjoyed singing but reminded me of a hoedown or community sing-along, not a series of musical prayers. Such services are often popular and appear to draw a lot of worshipers each Sunday, but they do not deepen people's understanding or raise the level of their commitment to God. They are mockeries of true worship, which always sets God front and center before everything and jealously guards the time for the Great Spirit.

Years ago, I heard Elam Davies, the famous Welsh preacher who became minister of the Fourth Presbyterian Church in Chicago, say that when he had completed his prayers for Sunday morning, he knelt down and offered them to God in the hope that they would draw people's souls to the Lord. When he had finished his sermon, he did the same with it. Wouldn't it be wonderful if we did the same with all the elements of our worship, including the greetings, the reading of Scripture, and even the announcements? What a difference it would make in the tone of our worship, and how greatly it would affect our lives over the years of our doing so!

43

Make a practice of seeking the advice of people with whom you wouldn't normally agree.

Sound hard? It really isn't, once you've become accustomed to doing it. And it has all sorts of benefits.

For one thing, it helps you to see aspects of a problem or proposal you might not otherwise see. People who think differently from us can often enrich our own vision by citing facts or opinions that help to correct or amend our own.

For another, it often helps to make friends of people who might otherwise be opposed to our ideas and proposals. Many of those who are most likely to oppose our leadership and ideas will be converted to allies by being included in the development of programs at the planning stage, so that they will feel some ownershp in them.

Additionally, seeking diverse opinions trains us to think in a broader scope and with greater clarity, since it means we have learned to examine things from beyond our own perspective.

It's really a win-win thing to do.

I didn't do it enough in my own pastorates. Looking back, I realize that I could have been more successful in several undertakings had I consulted with a few people before plowing ahead to accomplish them without benefit of my opponents' advice.

Once, for example, I talked to the deacons of a church I was pastoring about moving the 8:30 A.M. Sunday service from our enormous sanctuary into the much cozier and more comfortable chapel, where there would be a greater sense of community instead of the feeling of remoteness most of us felt under present conditions. I knew there were a couple of powerful men who would be opposed to the move, but I didn't bother to talk to them because they weren't the ones with the authority to grant the request.

One of the opponents of the move had a conniption fit and became very troublesome when the change was announced, and made no end of trouble about it. I might have avoided a lot of unpleasantness had I only talked to him and the other opponents before the move and asked them how they would have addressed our problem. One of them would probably have suggested the very move we made, and the matter would have gone much more smoothly.

44

Keep regular hours.

Most professionals do. They show up at their offices reasonably early, spend most of the day there, and leave reasonably late. Is there any reason the minister shouldn't do this too?

One of the Scottish ministers—I don't remember who now—used to say that he woke up to the sound of factory workers' boots on their way to work at 6 A.M., and he didn't feel right going back to sleep when his parishioners were out on the job, so he got up and went to his church early. Few of our church people start that early today, but, adjusting for the sociological changes, perhaps we ought to be thinking the same way.

I used to write my sermons at home, simply because I had become accustomed to working in my study while I was teaching at the university and was not comfortable composing sermons in my office at church. But except for that one morning a week, I was always at the church or on church-related business (visiting the hospital, calling in homes, attending meetings, etc.) from 8 A.M. till well after 5 P.M. every day.

I was a stickler about this for two reasons. One was that I had to set an example for the staff. If I didn't spend my day working where people could find me, they might well have assumed they could do the same. Another was that I wanted the church members to know they were getting their money's worth of my attention.

I know a highly placed minister who has been very lax about his time at the office, and he has produced a large number of subordinates whom members of his congregation complain are difficult to see or talk to at any time of the day. Now a new senior minister is replacing that minister, and he is going to have a hard time bringing discipline and order to a staff that has not been accustomed to it.

Dr. William Hinson, who was for many years the senior minister of the First United Methodist Church of Houston, once told me that he could not face the board of his congregation if he did not work as hard as or harder than the many executives of major companies who sat on the board. For him, there was no question about how many hours he should be at his church each week.

"I know the church is more than an institution," he said. "But part of it functions like an institution, and that means I have to live like a CEO."

45

Take a good, relaxing vacation at least once a year, and more often than that if you are in a large church with a lot of responsibilities.

No one should have to tell ministers this, but some forget how important it is to really get away and let their souls repair themselves, quite apart from how carefully they work at this all year.

Only a few doctors, I think, become as engrossed in their work as many pastors do. Most other professionals don't.

Think about it. The majority of ministers work at least six days a week. Even on their days off, they are brooding over their sermons and the problems they face in their counseling and other work. And most ministers work ten or twelve hours a day. They may come home at 5 P.M., but usually there's something to do in the evenings as well. If nothing else, they're thinking about their prayers and sermons for Sunday. They live under the burden of their weekly performance.

In smaller churches, two or three weeks of vacation time may be ample. But in churches of a thousand members or more, a minister needs twice that much time. Most ministers I know require at least a week of intensive vacation to decompress to the point where they can begin enjoying themselves and their families.

When I was a pastor in Lynchburg, Virginia, I often took three or four weeks' worth of vacation time in England. I did this because my wife and I loved England (we lived there for a year on at least two occasions) and because it was the only way I could get far enough from my parish that people didn't expect me to return for weddings and funerals.

For the first week, I merely vegetated, walking the streets of London, going to plays, and looking at bookstalls. Then, by the second week, I was ready to take a car and drive out in the country, traveling to Cornwall or walking in the Lake District. But—and I'm almost ashamed to admit this—I worked on sermons almost the whole time I was away, so that I invariably returned to America with five or six sermons virtually finished in my notebook. Otherwise, I knew, I would be swamped when I returned because of all the extra things that would pile up while I was away.

I really appreciate the laity in some churches I've heard about who all but demand that their pastors take time off. Some even go as far as to make reservations for them and make sure they get away at the appropriate time to take advantage of them.

Don't ever apologize for taking a vacation. As one friend said after he retired, "I needed six months of doing nothing to be able to get up in the morning and be glad I finally had nothing to do!"

46

Attend a good, solid ministers' conference at least once a year.

You'll be glad you did, and so will your congregation. Few things invigorate a minister more, or do more to stimulate the pastoral brain. The chance to sit in a congregation with other ministers and hear noted lecturers and preachers is one of the most refreshing things a hard-working minister can do.

There are a number of good conferences scattered all around the United States, plus a few good ones in the United Kingdom for those who want to travel abroad. Almost all of them feature the same kind of program: devotionals, worship, singing, Bible study, lectures on theology, sociology, ethics, and pastoral care, and opportunities for ministers to eat around the table and chat with one another about what's happening in their own parishes.

Many denominations sponsor such conferences primarily for the use of their own ministers, but I recommend finding a good ecumenical conference or two so that you meet some people who aren't mirror images of yourself. The Princeton Institute of Theology, for example, has been transforming ministers for decades, and it's close enough to New York that those who attend it are able to get into the big city for a breath of urban life and culture while they're there. There are also conferences at Oxford University and the University of Edinburgh for ministers who'd like to combine a professional getaway with a chance to travel abroad.

Some ministers report that the opportunity to visit new parts of the world, or even new areas of the United States, is as enriching to them as attending the sessions at their conferences. One minister from the southeastern United States told me, after attending his first conference in San Francisco, "Boy, I never saw anything like that Bay Area. For six months after I returned home, I could sit through a dull board meeting at my church by just dreaming of what it was like to watch the sailboats drifting under the Golden Gate Bridge at sunset!"

47

Once a year, make a list of all your sermon topics and texts for the past year and survey them to make sure you are cutting a wide enough swath with your preaching.

I knew an older minister who did something like this after moving to a new parish. He decided to review his sermons for the ten years at his last parish, partly in hopes of seeing what he could recycle in his new appointment.

"I set aside a whole afternoon to do this," he said. "To begin with, I cleared a big space in the living room, moving the furniture back against the walls, so I could stack my sermons on the floor according to text and topic. Then I began creating a new pile for each general subject area or text I had used.

"What I found astounded me. I needn't have cleared the room at all. The top of the coffee table would have been enough. "I learned that I had gone back to the same few subjects and texts again and again. I had a few tall stacks but not many stacks."

This is the reason some preachers like to follow the lectionary. It keeps them moving through the Bible via texts they wouldn't ordinarily use for their sermons.

Even they, however, often preach the same subject material in spite of using different texts. As soon as they have read and disposed of their texts in a very brief fashion, they head cross-country to their favorite topics, like a horse heading for the barn. I've heard members of a New York congregation say that their pastor, who had been with them for twenty-five years, had only six or eight sermons in his head and simply refitted them for every text and occasion.

This is why surveying your preaching topics and texts is important. It allows you to see how large your scope is, and whether you are being faithful to the needs of your congregation.

You might even want to develop a list of things you think your people need to hear—perhaps sermons about marriage, child-rearing, work, suffering, faith, science, friendship, kindness, character formation, death and dying, life after death, and end times—a sort of checklist you can follow in planning future sermons. That way you have a real commitment to casting your net more widely and touching upon the many things your members ought to be learning about the Christian faith.

48

Keep a registry in which you enter the dates and names of all the baptisms, confirmations, marriages, and funerals you perform, and brief notes on all the persons you counsel.

I didn't do this and have often wished I did. As it is, I have to thumb back through my journals to find names and dates when I need to know them. It would be much handier to have all the information consolidated in a single book and in chronological order.

People seldom ask for such information, but occasionally a minister will be requested to provide details about the date or fact of a baptism, marriage, or funeral, and a central repository is then a very convenient resource.

Even more importantly, ministers who keep such a registry can occasionally look back through it and be reminded of various people and events in their ministries, which provides an overview of the number of people whose lives they have been a part of through the years.

One minister who retired a few months ago told me that he has spent two or three afternoons when it was too rainy to play golf just leafing through his records and recalling all the people he has been privileged to know.

"I feel a surge of good will when I do it," he said. "It reminds me that I have been a part of a lot of people's pains and joys, that I was there for them when they needed me. People can't imagine how good that makes me feel. I know I have been . . . well, useful."

49

Live modestly—which, in your case, means not living above the level of your median-income families.

In other words, don't live in the best house in your neighborhood or drive a fancier car than most of your parishioners.

This is a matter of some sensitivity, especially in smaller towns and communities where everybody knows everybody else's business. I grew up in a town where one of the local ministers married the daughter of a wealthy businessman. People thought well of this minister because he never made any show of his new economic status, but continued to wear modestly priced suits and drive a median-priced Chevrolet.

By contrast, a well-known evangelist from Fort Smith, Arkansas, named Angel Martinez was widely reputed to live above his station as a minister, buying expensive clothes and flashy cars. His explanation for his "weakness" was that he grew up in poverty in Mexico and was making up for the fact that he didn't even have a pair of shoes to wear when he left home at eighteen to accept a scholarship at an American university.

Once, Martinez was scheduled to hold a revival meeting in the small town where a friend of mine was a pastor. The pastor was impressed by his thoughtfulness when he telephoned a few days before the meeting to ask what kind of automobiles most of his parishioners drove.

"Why, Fords and Chevrolets, mostly," said the pastor.

"Ah," said Martinez, "then I'd better leave my Lincoln Continental at home when I come, and drive my little car."

The pastor thanked him for his consideration and said he looked forward to his arrival.

The next week, Martinez drove into town in a passionate-purple Porsche!

Of course, it is not really anyone else's business what size house you live in or what kind of car you drive. But many members of your congregation will prefer you to exhibit a certain modesty in your tastes and desires, just as they will care whether you've been married more than once or have a problem with alcohol. *C'est la vie*, as the French say—that's life!

50

Always remember that the church you pastor is God's church, not yours, and after that it is the people's church. You are only a servant in their church and not its owner or its master.

Some of us forget this and begin to think, after we've been in a pastorate for a few years, that we have proprietary rights. We don't. Our only title is to the ministry, not the church.

I have seen several long-time pastors behave miserably when the time came for them to retire and leave their positions because they felt so proprietary that they were more than a little reluctant to turn them over to other ministers.

One, questioned about how he felt about another minister who had been called to replace him, slapped the table at which he was dining, making the china and silverware rattle, and said in a loud voice, "It is *my* church and *I* will decide when I'm ready to turn it over to someone else!" Another, feeling hostile toward a fellow minister who had been brought in by his board to help him through his retirement, shouted, "This is *my* church and I will not leave until I am ready to leave!"

It can only be supposed that when an older minister expresses his sense of proprietorship in such forceful terms it is because he has been seduced, from a much earlier time, into thinking of the pastorate as his, not God's and not the congregation's.

It is a healthy idea for new ministers, from the very first, to think of the church as belonging exclusively to God, not to you, so you don't ever reach this unattractive stage of attachment and delusion. That way you will not take any important step without first consulting God and until you are convinced it is what God would approve.

And if there is ever a contest between your will and the congregation's, you will remember that you are only temporarily the pastor of their church and many of them will be there long after you have gone, so their vote, unless you have an absolute mandate from God, counts for more than yours.

51

Honor your spouse and your children, for you have put them in a tough situation.

It is an honored situation, to be sure, but they are thrust into a spotlight created by your being the pastor, and living in a spotlight is never easy. Ministers' wives—I'm not sure about ministers' husbands—have often been known to develop psychosomatic problems because of the stress they are under, and it is something of a miracle when ministers' children turn out normal and happy after growing up in a fishbowl.

My wife and I had one understanding in the pastorate: she would not do or say anything on Sunday that I would have to deal with on Monday. Otherwise, she was free to be herself.

But if I were doing my ministries over again, one thing I would do differently would be to pay more public compliments to my wife. Looking back, I realize what a treasure she was, and how much she helped me to be a successful pastor. She undertook many important roles in my churches and supported me in ways I probably never understood.

We have often been told that one of the significant aspects of our shared ministry was the way people could tell we loved one another. "It made us feel good," some have said years later, "just to see you come into a room holding hands and glowing at one another. It lifted our hopes for relationships with our own spouses, and set a model for our children as well."

It bothers us when we go to church and hear a minister allude to his or her spouse in a less-than-positive way. Not long ago, for example, we heard a pastor explaining something in his sermon. He said, "Now that isn't complicated, is it? I worried about saying it, because earlier I read this sermon to my wife and she had a hard time getting it. I told her again and again what it meant, and she still couldn't grasp it. But I just thought, 'Well, that's my wife. *They'll* understand it.'"

The minister's wife was sitting in the congregation. What he said had to be embarrassing to her on at least some level. She probably wanted to kill him because it was unnecessarily demeaning.

A good rule of thumb is this: always be as thoughtful and appreciative of your spouse and children as you would be of anyone else in the congregation. In fact, be *more* thoughtful and appreciative of them.

52

Always be prepared.

You don't have to have been a Boy Scout to make preparedness your motto as the minister of one of God's churches. But there are no two ways about it: every minister should be thoroughly prepared for everything he or she purports to do for the kingdom of God.

I know it looks sort of cool, as the young people say, to be casual about our work as ministers—to saunter into the pulpit on Sunday morning with a devil-may-care attitude about whether we have our sermons under our belts and are ready to preach, or to mosey into an important meeting without having given any thought to the agenda, or to show up only moments before a dinner where we are to give the invocation is about to get under way.

But to those who live their lives with a modicum of discipline and decency, this kind of inattention to our tasks is little short of sacrilegious. "Faithful in little things, faithful in the big ones," they think—and vice versa.

A lot of young people going into ministry have the idea that it is a soft life. They like being around the church, they know church people are among the kindest in the world, and they imagine themselves living a life of leisure. But the truth is that the church has its institutional side and every minister is expected to be a good manager of time and responsibilities, so preparation and discipline are important.

Think of it this way: slovenliness and disorder are of the devil and they belong to the chaos out of which God made the world; the kingdom is the essence of order and decency. So every time we fail to be prepared, we are contributing to the devil's cause, not God's.

53

Preach stewardship all the time.

Most ministers are expected to preach about money once a year, when it's time for the annual stewardship drive. But that's a little false, if you think about it. If stewardship is really important, then it ought to be woven into the fabric of everything we do—not with dollar signs, but with a sense that *everything* belongs to God.

That's a large part of what Christianity is about, isn't it? That everything about us is God's, and when we heard the good news of Jesus Christ, it turned our hearts around and we wanted to give it all back to God, keeping nothing for ourselves but what we need to live.

For St. Luke, this was the heart of the gospel. Over and over, in his Gospel, he stressed the way people's lives were changed when they met Jesus, and how they went away in sadness if they weren't prepared to give up everything to follow him.

Is it any different for us? Don't we want to say with the disciples, "Lord, we have left all to follow thee" (Luke 18:28)?

If we are serious about following, and the church we serve is serious, then there is an element of giving up what we have every time we congregate, repeat the Lord's Prayer, and sing a hymn of worship. There is a reminder of sacrifice every time we preach. And there is an opportunity to show this to God every time the ushers take up an offering.

I know the members of an average church don't all look at their privileges this way. They have to be wheedled and cajoled into parting with money for the upkeep of the church and its ministries. But that is the challenge, to teach those folks about their responsibilities as

Christ's followers and the spiritual rewards that stem from giving everything to God.

This is what I mean by preaching stewardship all the time. It ought not to be a once- or twice-a-year exercise. It's actually part of the warp and woof of every service of worship, every sermon, every prayer, every hymn, even every announcement. So do it!

54

Take time to be with people—real time, really being with them.

I hate to think that any minister doesn't do this. But I know from my own experience how busy ministers rarely think they have the time to be leisurely with everybody. Most of us live on skates, racing from one thing to another.

One of my real idols in this regard was Bill Gray. Dr. William Gray was pastor of the Downtown Presbyterian Church in Nashville when I taught at Vanderbilt. He was kind of a hoot, and I often heard stories about him. Sometimes they were about how kind and patient he was with his parishioners.

Like the time he went to visit in a home where someone had died. The family was huddled in the living room with the undertaker, making basic decisions about the time of the funeral, when to look at coffins, where the burial would be, and so on. They apologized to Bill and asked if he'd like to come back later. He said not to mind him, he'd just go out to the kitchen and make himself a cup of coffee.

He did. There was a morning newspaper there, so he sat and read it. Then he washed up the dishes that were in the sink. The family had forgotten he was there. Finally someone remembered and said, "Oh gosh, Dr. Gray is here!" He was having another cup of coffee when they went to look for him, and he was as calm as if he'd just arisen from a nap.

It wasn't that Bill didn't have a busy parish. He did. It was, as its name implies, right smack in the middle of downtown Nashville. It had a dozen programs for the poor, the homeless, overstressed businesspersons, young people, Grand Ole Opry wannabees, and others. And Bill was often in demand as a speaker. He had a radio program on Sunday mornings, and people from hundreds of miles around Nashville tuned in to hear him. Many of them wrote or called him afterwards.

But Bill grasped the most essential thing about pastoral care, the fact that a pastor has to *be there* for a parishioner in a moment of crisis. His waiting patiently in that kitchen for two hours that morning was more important than anything else he had to do. He would have done it even if the president of the United States had been waiting for him back at his office.

55

Read widely in genres and subjects that have nothing ostensibly to do with your religion.

It is tempting, of course, to confine one's reading and study to the things that have immediate bearing upon one's work. Ministers therefore tend to be rather narrowly focused on religion—on sermons, prayer, pastoral care, and church work in general.

But if it is true, as someone once said, that the art of preaching is to prepare a preacher and deliver that, then it is very important for every minister to widen his or her scope as much as possible in order to be as fully informed a person as possible.

I have always been grateful that, for whatever reasons, I took a PhD in literature before going to seminary, because acquaintance with the great classics of British and American literature, with some French and German thrown in, has been an immeasurable source of knowledge and understanding to me. And I have often envied other ministers who had a similar background in such fields as science, psychology, and sociology.

The fact is, the more we know, in whatever field of human knowledge and expertise, the more we have to offer our people as pastors and commentators on the faith.

Ministers who haven't been to graduate school in some area outside religion shouldn't feel bad that they lack this extra "reach" as ministers. They have their whole lifetimes to make up for whatever lacunae exist in their understanding. All they have to do is undertake a reading program that will fill in those blanks in their backgrounds.

I suggest making regular trips to a good secular bookstore or the local library and bringing home a few books that look appealing and starting to read them. The best pastors and preachers I know have done this most of their ministries, and the difference it makes in their work and personalities is evidence of the good it has done them.

You can focus in on a particular area you'd like to be more knowledgeable about, such as art, literature, theater, science, or psychology; or you can choose to be eclectic, and spread yourself over many areas.

Consider such titles as Stephen Hawking's *A Brief History of Time*, Thomas Moore's *The Care of the Soul*, Sherwin Nuland's *How We Die*, Edwin Friedman's *Generation to Generation,* and Daniel Goleman's *Emotional Intelligence*. Or, among literary works, the poetry of Emily Dickinson, Wallace Stevens, and Gerard Manley Hopkins; the essays of Wendell Berry and Loren Eiseley; and the novels of Cormac McCarthy, Rosamunde Pilcher, and Nikos Kazantzakis.

The point is, there is an absolute wealth of reading material just waiting on the bookshelves for you, and there is very little of it that won't deepen and enrich both your existence and your ministry. Author John Updike once said that he couldn't resist going into a bookstore he was passing because he knew there was a book in there that was going to change his life! You'll probably have a similar experience.

56

Don't take yourself too seriously and you won't be too disappointed when others don't.

Being a minister is enough to give most of us a big head. Imagine standing in front of all those people every week and being given an opportunity to speak your mind without interruption for fifteen or twenty minutes. Why, it's enough to make anyone think too highly of him or herself, isn't it?

There is nothing worse than ministers who let their positions assume undue importance in relation to their sense of self. As someone has put it, they become legends in their own minds.

A Scottish writer told about a pastor who went into the pulpit so full of himself that he exuded an overpowering sense of self-confidence. But he did such a poor job with the sermon that he looked quite dispirited when he came down. "Ach," said one of his parishioners, "if ye'd only gone up as ye came down, ye might've come down as ye went up."

Bear in mind that you are only an ordinary mortal whom God has seen fit to call into the ministry, not an immortal who is likely to be remembered for more than a few years when you are gone. Try to keep a reasonable perspective on your life and its very small, almost infinitesimal space in the long history of Christianity filled with saints, bishops, and martyrs.

And you might want to remember President Franklin Roosevelt, who, during the intense days of World War II, spent an evening discussing strategy with a top aide. Finally they went out to sit in the Rose Garden under the vast, starry sky before turning in.

"Ah," said Roosevelt at last, "I think we feel small enough now to go in and go to bed."

57

Do everything possible to avoid turning your pulpit into a political platform.

You will sometimes be tempted to advise people how to think about a particular political candidate or proposition. Please try to refrain! It is wise not to take sides, even when you aren't in the pulpit.

I know one minister who merely attended a Democratic Party function in his Republican community, was inadvertently photographed, and a few days later saw his picture in the local newspaper, where his church members also saw it. He was gone from that pastorate within two months.

Remember that the IRS takes a dim view of any church that appears to be endorsing a political candidate. Several churches have lost their tax-exempt status because their pastors spoke out for one candidate or another, or allowed other persons to enter the pulpit for the purpose of endorsing a candidate.

But a higher principle is at stake. Ever since the days of Paul the Apostle, who advised the Romans not to speak out against their governing authorities (Rom 13:1-7), it has been considered appropriate for pastors of Christian churches to remain above politics. Their fealty is to heaven, not earthly parties or propositions.

58

Be gracious about receiving the gifts members of your congregation want to give you.

Most people truly love their ministers, even if the ministers don't deserve it, and they like to do nice things for them. It makes them feel good. Their ministers become outlets for their most generous impulses. What was it Luther said—we need the beggars because they help us to give things away? Well, ministers do the same thing for a lot of parishioners. They elicit gifts.

Learn to accept these gifts with charm and gratitude.

Oh, I know you may feel that they compromise your integrity. And it's true that some people like to buy things with their gifts, and will later expect you to be on their side in any quarrel or debate.

But consider what being able to give a gift to the minister does for the average church person. It primes the pump of that person's generosity and produces a good feeling that may even extend to other parts of the person's life. It satisfies the donor's need for more contact with the minister, the desire for greater visibility in the pastor's eyes.

When I think back on my career at the many gifts people have given me—books, magazines, candy, flowers, meals, play tickets, a ham or turkey at Thanksgiving, the occasional use of a condo in a recreation area—I see happy faces and remember those persons' delight at being able to reach out to me and my family. I can't recall a single ulterior motive I imagined they had—only a sense of joy and pleasure at being able to do something nice for their minister.

I'm sure there would have been a limit to what I would have accepted. For example, I couldn't have taken the $150,000 golf course membership
a friend of mine received, or any of the three houses a famous minister from Houston was given over the course of several years. But the other things were not a problem, for they weren't big enough to create a sense of limitless obligation.

I haven't forgotten the nice things people did, and I never let them forget them either. Years later, I have reminded them. Sometimes they themselves have forgotten. But being reminded has revived the worth of the gift, and they have received a kind of half-life benefit from having given it.

59

Be careful whom you allow to share your pulpit.

In most churches, it is the minister who holds control over who does or doesn't speak from the pulpit, so it is the minister's job to be very sure that the speaker is a person of integrity and true worthiness.

Some ministers are careful to secure pulpit supplies who are less capable and interesting than themselves, thereby ensuring that their congregation won't say, "Hey, that supply preacher was tremendous! Why don't we get her to be our pastor?"

Maybe a good rule of thumb is to ask yourself, *Would I want to go to church and hear this person I'm asking to take my place when I'm away?* If the answer is *yes, definitely,* then that person is a good choice. But if the answer is *no, I don't think so,* dismiss the thought and find a better substitute.

I have always admired the humble pastor who is happy to secure the very best preachers available to fill the pulpit during an illness or vacation. It shows that this pastor has the Spirit of God in his or her heart and actually puts the kingdom of God above personal interests.

One of the finest compliments anyone ever paid me was one given by a plainspoken man who was an usher in one of my parishes. "Pastor," he said, "you sure do get us some fine speakers when you're away. Don't get me wrong, I like listening to you. But it's always nice to hear a fresh voice once in a while, and you always provide us with the best ones."

60

Visit, visit, visit.

How much depends in part on where your ministry is located, of course. Pastors in metropolitan areas find it almost too time-consuming to do a lot of home and office calls. Those in small towns and rural areas can do a lot more. But there isn't a pastor around who doesn't need to hear this tip: visiting your flock is one of the most important things you do.

There are privacy issues. It's hard to get into apartment houses unless you've called ahead, and many folks don't like you just showing up at their door unannounced. So it's a good idea to go out with a plan. Have your secretary set up visits a day or two in advance, so people will be prepared for your coming. Or call them on your cell phone as you make your rounds, giving them ample notice of your arrival.

But for every person who is rankled by your interrupting their day, four will treasure your interest and the time they have with you. And the person who feels rankled may even relent and inwardly admit that it was nice the pastor thought of them.

Years later, I remember with great fondness my visits to certain parishioners, notably some of the little old ladies and gents who didn't get out of their homes very much. It was always an occasion when the pastor came to call. You could tell that the excitement ratio went up, and they flurried around to arrange a cup of tea or a plate of cookies to set on the coffee table. Even now, the memory of those smiling, upturned faces lifts my spirits.

Office hours are important too, and every pastor ought to have a set time when people know they can come to discuss a problem or merely to get to know the pastor better. But for most parishioners, the fact that the pastor has seen them in their own habitat gives them a feeling of comfort. If anything happens to them or somebody they love, the pastor will know where to come and won't feel like a stranger.

Be sure to take calling cards when you go to visit. If there's no one at home, leave your card with a personal note on the back. For the person who missed you, it's the next best thing to having the visit. And you can bet that the card won't be thrown away. It'll turn up years hence as a bookmark in something they were reading at the time, or tucked into the pages of the Bible, and even then it will be good for a little thanksgiving.

61

Lavish some regular attention on your body.

Of course you're in a spiritual business, but you surely know that bodies and spirits are inextricably commingled. When your body is out of shape, your soul isn't all it ought to be. And it works the other way too.

Too many pastors are overweight and out of shape. They can plead extenuating circumstances—too much to do, no gym to in which to work out, people always poking food at them, the need for comfort food, and so on. But those are only excuses.

Most of us could walk a lot more than we do. Try parking the car a few blocks from your parishioner's home or office, so you have to cover the distance on foot. Take the stairs, not the elevator, when you call on people at the hospital. If your church offices are on several floors, always take the stairs there too.

We all have different body structures and different rates of metabolism, so this isn't a matter of whether we're slender or fat, slack or muscular. It's about having a healthy body in which to nourish our healthy souls.

One pastor told me that the best investment he ever made was a week at a health spa where he fed on salads, tofu, and fruit swirls, spent hours on the treadmill and in a sauna, had massages and training sessions, ran around an indoor track, swam, and generally toned up his soul's casing. He planned to make it a semi-annual occurrence, figuring he owed it to himself after the abuses to which he subjected his body in the course of his work.

"Besides," he said, "I've never done anything that gave me more ideas for sermons!"

Be technologically savvy.

Learn to use a computer. Get a cell phone. Figure out how to text message. "Live-stream" your worship service. Create podcasts for iPods.

We live in an electronic environment today, and the pastor who hasn't got the hang of it is penalized by missing out on a lot of communication. Imagine, when radios were invented, not having one; or, when televisions became the rage, not getting one of those. It isn't a matter of trying to be more spiritual by not using electronic gadgets. It's more serious than that. It's a matter of being out of touch in an ultra-connected world.

I'm one to talk. For years, after everybody had a personal computer, my secretary fussed at me for writing my sermons on an old-fashioned typewriter and handing them to her to process. When I left that pastorate, one of my going-away gifts was a Radio Shack computer. I set it up in my study at the next pastorate, but never took the time to learn to use it. When I left that pastorate for a university professorship, I figured it was time to catch up with the times. Only by then, my computer was two or three generations out of date, so I had to junk it and get a new setup.

But I watch my electronically savvy friends using their gadgets to enhance their ministries, and I envy them. They receive calls on their cell phones while driving to meetings or to visit parishioners; they text message people they can't reach; they blog to their members; they put their worship services and special meditations on live-stream.

One pastor who is a child of this age sends me his weekly e-message to the congregation. It is beautifully formatted and always lively, thoughtful, and provocative. He makes a lot of typos and grammatical slips (which means he doesn't hand the text to a secretary to send out) but that only enhances the charm and sense of directness in his messages. I feel an instant rapport because I know it is him, it is the guy writing the message. He comes through loud and clear. I can only imagine that the members of his flock appreciate these communications as if they were a personal call from the pastor, because they have the dew of freshness and relevance on them. My hat is off to this pastor. He's really with it!

63

Pick your fights.

Uh-oh! Am I condoning the pastor's fighting in church? Yes and no. I'm not a spiritual pugilist, but I'm a realist, and I know that no pastor can always avoid putting up the dukes against certain parishioners who set themselves against the wishes and welfare of the congregation. You can be the most passive person in the world and sometimes still not be able to avoid a struggle with those who are determined to be your enemies or the church's enemies.

A pastor is lost, though, when he or she becomes a steady combatant. If we're living in the Spirit of God (which hopefully we are) we want peace and love, not quarreling and contentiousness. We don't want our spirits perpetually disturbed by living in a state of battle readiness.

So what do we do?

First, we try to live above the fray as much as possible. We overlook ugly remarks and walk past most of the fights. We keep our minds on heavenly things and we forgive a lot. We pray for our enemies.

Then, if it ever comes to it, we are reduced to strategizing—to thinking like a general who doesn't have many troops and is facing an enemy eager to join battle. The question is, *How can I put a lid on this thing or else finish it off quickly, so the effects of the battle don't spill over on others or cause a bigger row than already exists?*

In my experience, it is always good to pray about one's enemies and what they are up to, thereby setting the situation before God and asking for guidance about what to do. I've seldom been advised, in such a time of prayer, to go for the throat and finish off an enemy. If I've ever done that, it was on my own, not because God led me to do it.

Occasionally, prayer or no prayer, there seems to be nothing else we can do except stand up to a bully and face the bully down (I didn't say "him" because there are a lot of female bullies too).

When this happens, we need to be so filled with the Spirit that we can speak calmly and decisively to the enemy, say what we believe needs to be said, make any retributive threats that must be made, and try to put a cap on the volcano before it explodes. If it explodes anyway, then we know we have done our very best to prevent it and aren't to blame for what has happened. But we can still pray for the people who couldn't live in peace with us.

64

Do beautiful weddings for the sons and daughters of your parish.

They take a lot of time and involve a lot of input, but they're a wonderful gift from the pastor to his or her parish. Don't think of them as intrusions—I heard one minister complain that he wished his sanctuary weren't so beautiful and fewer people wanted to be married in it—but as opportunities to minister.

If you're a gifted liturgist with a talent for language, write your own services and adapt them to suit the particular weddings you're conducting. If you're not, find some lovely model services and use them. But be sure to adapt them to the local situation and the couple being married.

Have each service printed up in a beautiful copy you can give to the couple after you've married them. Inscribe it with a few words of heartfelt love and best wishes and sign your name. Some couples will be taking them out to reread during their anniversaries as long as twenty or thirty years later.

You can do a lot in your prewedding counseling to get the marriage off on a good foot. If you don't have any skill in this area, find a fellow minister who can instruct you. My grandfather, who was a farmer, used to say, "You can't do much to straighten a furrow once you've started plowing it." So it's very important to get a marriage off right, and you're the person to do it.

These days, when many rehearsal and wedding dinners too often turn into ribald occasions in which the male and female attendants try to shock the older people present by narrating embarrassing personal stories about the bride and groom, set a high tone by gathering the attendants before the dinner to have a prayer with them and remind them that there is something sacred about weddings and therefore about all the related festivities as well.

During the wedding itself, you can help the families that have been so busy putting together a monumental occasion to remember the holy aspects of what the bride and groom are doing, and to feel in the end that it was all worthwhile because there was such a spiritual atmosphere about the wedding itself. You are the only one who can do this, so do it thoughtfully and do it well. Like Christ at Cana of Galilee, turn the ordinary water of each wedding occasion into the finest wine anybody has ever tasted!

65

Personalize funerals and turn them into occasions for spiritual celebration.

Someone described going to a funeral for a close friend that was held in an Episcopalian church. The priest read the service for the dead from the Book of Common Prayer. The man said, "He didn't even mention my deceased friend's name. I felt like going up, staring at the corpse, and saying, 'I had to make sure it was who I thought it was, because I haven't heard a darned thing since I got here that told me whose funeral I was attending!'"

For many friends and family members of a deceased parishioner, performing that parishioner's funeral is one of the most important services you will ever do, regardless of how long your pastorate in their church is. Therefore it should be done with grace, thoughtfulness, tact, and beauty.

Personalize the service by including everything you can that will recall the essence of the deceased person's personality. If it is someone you haven't known very intimately, as often happens if you haven't been the person's pastor very long, make a point of going to the home before you prepare the service to talk with family members and others about who the person was in life. They may begin slowly, not certain it is all right to talk freely about the recently dead, but will almost always warm to their subject as they go along. Someone in the family will begin recalling characteristic stories from years ago. There will be laughter as well as tears. Draw upon all of this to compose your

prayers and remarks for the service. Death itself will sacralize the occasion, but it is up to you to sound the right notes that will humanize it
and make it a celebration of *this* person's life and death instead of life
and death in general.

Don't be afraid of injecting humor into a funeral service. Humor is
part of life, and you are dealing with the whole of life, not merely
death and sadness. It is the other parts of life that make death and sadness more tolerable. A little laughter in the service makes the whole
event more beautiful.

Remember, in the funeral liturgy, that it is God we adore, and
orient the prayers and remarks in such a way as to remind people that
you are setting everything under the aspect of eternity. Nothing else
will turn the sadder, more unbearable aspects of death and celebration
into the joyous notes of spiritual victory.

66

Never neglect your own church for work in the denomination or a parachurch organization.

It feels very rewarding to be able to hold a denominational office or be a big shot in some other Christian organization, because it is a great compliment to be recognized by people in larger institutional circles for our talents and abilities. But keep a realistic perspective as you yield to entreaties from these larger entities, remembering who pays your salary and that a lot of your people will not be happy if you are away too much or tend to neglect your local duties for the unpaid ones.

Pastors in connectional churches, such as the Episcopal or United Methodist, are most vulnerable to being suborned for duties away from their own flocks. The bishops and superintendents in these organizations seem to think that the "wheels within wheels" of Ezekiel's vision were a prediction of how it should be in the church, so are never happier than when they are conscripting pastors and associate pastors to keep those wheels turning.

A good rule of thumb for any pastor is the 80/20 one. Keep 80 percent of your weight in your local church assignment and never permit more than 20 percent of it to be drawn into the orbit of the larger church. If you violate this rule and begin to allot your time and effort, say, 60/40 or 50/50, you might want to consider that it is time to become a field officer and not a local pastor.

There is a saying that "all politics is local." That's very true, and never truer than for a pastor when it comes to where the pastor should devote his or her greatest time and energy. No great preachers, no great pastoral counselors, and no great church administrators are ever made at the general level—only in the local parish.

I cannot remember having ever heard a pastor say, "I just gave up my church to be an administrator in the denomination, and I couldn't be happier!" But I have heard numerous pastors remark, "Thank God, I've just gotten out of my responsibilities as a denominational officer and can concentrate on my own parish, which is where I've always wanted to be!"

Maybe you'd like to ask yourself this question: *If I were to die today, where would I be missed the most, in my church or in the denomination?* Few of us would have to struggle to answer that.

67

At least nine times out of ten, your child's birthday party or your spouse's trip to the doctor is a greater priority for you than a deacon's meeting or almost anything else that's happening at church.

Don't feel guilty about making the choice!

A lot of ministers are good at laying guilt trips on themselves (and their families) about their duties. If there's a conflict between something personal and something at the church, they usually fly a white flag without any thought of protest.

But being a pastor doesn't mean that you don't have a life of your own or that you don't owe your family as much consideration as you would if you were a bricklayer, a school teacher, or a taxi driver. It's as important to protect your private relationships as it is your public ones. Otherwise, you'll end up being a professional without a private dimension to your existence.

Most people in your congregation will understand the nature of your choices and applaud you for honoring your family. They know your family suffers a lot of times from your being so often in the public arena, and they will thank you for remembering to be a real father or mother, wife or husband, and not just a paper saint.

Think about this: you're probably going to be the pastor of your church less than four years (which is more than the national average for pastoral tenures). You're going to be a husband or wife, father or mother, for a lot longer than that!

68

Never preach out of anger, only out of love.

Sounds easy, right? There will be times when it isn't. There will be a day when somebody has just insulted or attacked you, and you will go into the pulpit thinking you'd like to see that person boiled in oil. Or somebody will have finked out on an important mission, leaving you holding the bag, and you will get up to preach with that person sitting a few rows away, so that it will be hard to resist reaching out and strangling them.

At such moments, all you can do is kick back into the Spirit, forget about the human pressures, and preach to all those other dear people who are longing to hear the gospel for their hungry, desperate souls. Put the anger on hold and deal with it later. But don't take it into the pulpit with you.

Maybe it's a good thing to remember that it isn't your pulpit, and being the minister doesn't give you the right to spout off in it about something that's eating you up but has nothing to do with the rest of the congregation.

Think about a grade-school teacher who must give a lesson on addition and subtraction just after having had a run-in with the principal. She's mad as hops at being told she has to show up for a parent-teacher meeting that somebody else was supposed to cover and she had tickets to a hockey match. What does she do? Reprimand the kids for what the principal did? No way. She swallows her anger so the children don't think she's mad at them—it's hard enough learning math without thinking the teacher's angry with you—and calmly, sweetly, and patiently goes on with the lesson she'd planned.

That's what you have to do as a pastor. You do your job without dragging your personal beef into it.

Who knows? You may feel so uplifted by the service that it deflates your anger.

69

Get to know everybody in your flock, even if you have a big church.

A friend of mine belonged to a medium-sized church. Her pastor had been in that church for five years. She met him in the grocery store one day and they locked eyes over the produce. She said she could see his mind churning, thinking, "I know that woman from somewhere. She must be a member of my congregation. But darned if I know who she is. I'll have to fake it."

He spoke and they chatted about the vegetables. His voice was very upbeat and assuring, but he never did figure out who she was. She said she wasn't about to tell him and make it easy for him. When she started to move away, he said cheerily, "Well, see you on Sunday, I hope."

"Sure," she said, knowing he still didn't have a clue.

Was it okay that her pastor didn't know her after five years? Most of us probably have parishioners we can't call by name after that long. Some people don't recall names easily, or put names and faces together with ease. But it sure would have been nice if he had known her, wouldn't it?

What to do?

Most churches have a membership book with photographs. If they don't, they should. Several photography companies happily agree to provide them free for the membership if, in return, they are permitted to solicit the congregation to purchase private photographs from the ones they've taken.

If your church has such a book, get it even before you arrive in the parish. Study it the way you'd study for the SATs or a law exam. You can even cut up the book, carry a few pages with you, and cram during your spare time while waiting at the dentist's office or standing in line at the pharmacy.

If the church doesn't have such a valuable treasure for you, carry your digital camera around with you for a few weeks and explain to people that you'd like to take their picture so you can remember them the next time you meet them. They'll understand that. Most people have trouble with names and faces of people they've known only a brief time. In fact, they'll applaud you for taking so much trouble to try to learn who they are.

Later, after a reasonable time, if you run into a church member and can't remember their name, you might want to write them a note after you've checked your pictures and say, "I really hated it that I couldn't recall your name when we met earlier today. I feel like such a failure. My brain is just overwhelmed right now. I hope you'll forgive me."

Ninety-nine times out of a hundred, that'll buy you a lot of grace.

70

If you have a secretary, be sure this person has a warm Christian spirit and loves your parish- ioners, because that's better than being a good typist.

I know a church that has a barracuda for a pastor's secretary. She's really a witch. She seems to resent anybody's bothering her for anything and often barks at people on the phone. She pretends to be guarding the minister's time and privacy, but what she's really doing is systematically alienating the congregation.

Personally, I was very lucky always to have an excellent secretary who had a warm, gracious spirit as well. As I told each one of them, I couldn't have done my job without them. They were more valuable than rubies and fine gold. They could smooth troubled waters, track down lost souls, and charm cobras out of their baskets.

But I have heard horror stories from ministers who inherited Hilda the Hun and didn't know how to get rid of her. One pastor was so intimidated by his secretary that he often waited until she was out of her office to sneak into his. Another said that having to deal with his was like having a root canal and brain surgery—at the same time.

The most promising thing in a case like this is to have a personnel committee that can take care of the matter—replacing Hilda the

Hun—without your becoming personally involved. If there isn't such a committee in your church, you should undertake to get one as soon as possible, and *then* arrange for Hilda's departure.

One friend of mine had a Herman the Hun, a male secretary he had employed because he felt sorry for the man, who hadn't been able to find work. Herman turned out to be a terrible secretary. His worst fault was bearing tales about the pastor to some little old ladies who didn't like the pastor anyway. When my friend learned this, he asked his personnel committee to do a review of Herman's work and determine whether they should retain his services. The review was negative and Herman was asked to leave.

Knowing the pastor was behind his forced leaving, Herman became angry and said he was going to get a gun and kill the pastor. He was so convincing about this threat that the pastor had to turn over his responsibilities to an associate minister and go into hiding for several weeks.

So personnel committees aren't always the answer. But usually they are.

71

Always make a big deal of recognizing your people for their achievements.

This goes for everybody from high school graduates and beauty-contest winners to somebody who has published a poem or had their photograph published in the local newspaper.

Most people crave identity. That's one reason some of them join the church, so they'll have a family of folks who recognize and embrace them when they attend. If we can help them enhance their sense of identity and make them feel welcome at the same time, it's a win-win situation.

Smart pastors often work something about their parishioners into their sermons—a note of commendation, a recognition of worth, a little story about their contagious spirit of joy or heroism. This only takes half a minute, and it means an hour's worth of praise and warmth to the person of whom we speak.

Imagine what it does for some lonely little boy or girl to be mentioned in a service. Or, for that matter, any shy wallflower of an adult who rarely gets in the limelight for anything.

When I was preaching at Marble Church in New York, I did this for a woman in the congregation who had given me a book. I used an illustration from the book, and in introducing it, thanked the woman by name for having been the instrument by which I came to the story. Friends said she puffed up with pride at having been acknowledged, and it wasn't long afterward that she asked me if I would conduct her memorial service when she died. It meant that much to her.

Maybe churches should have an annual Recognition Day, a time for lifting up numerous people in the congregation who have had special attainments of any kind during the year. The worst part of that, of course, would be a failure to acknowledge someone who really deserved it or thought they did. But maybe that could be offset by saying in the course of the service that there are many unsung heroes who ought to be honored, and asking if there are members who want to stand right then to acknowledge something that has gone unheralded.

72

Be a good sport.

Even if you aren't a "hail-fellow-well-met," you can at least try to be open to exposure in different settings in your church, so that people know you would like to be a normal human being and not a self-righteous clergyperson. Stepping out from behind the clerical mask occasionally is actually good for your clerical image.

I fondly remember one of my pastors at a time when I was working in academia. He seemed somewhat stiff in the pulpit, but when I joined a church softball team, I found that he was already a member, and I got to know him much better on the ball field than I did on Sundays. It was great to see him in a role where he could really be himself.

Robert McCracken, minister at Riverside Church in New York, once told the story of a young Scottish minister who had become the new pastor of a small city congregation. He was pleased when the youth group of the church asked him to take part in a play they were producing but didn't think it proper for a clergyman to be seen on the stage. They continued to issue the request and promised it would be a small part so he wouldn't have to take much time from his parish duties to learn his lines.

Finally, elated at the attention, he agreed.

He was asked to speak only one line, but at a very dramatic moment. He was to enter a room, surprising a villain in his act of villainy. The villain would turn, pull out a gun, and shoot him. The minister would say, "My God, I'm shot!" and collapse to the floor. Simple. The minister said he could do that, but he insisted on amending the line from "My God, I'm shot!" to a more suitable "My goodness, I'm shot!" which he thought would be unlikely to offend even the strictest Puritan in his church.

The night of the play, the entire parish turned out, having heard that the new dominie was in the cast.

When his moment arrived, the minister walked onto the stage, surprised the villain, and was shot, all as planned. But the villain, being an enterprising fellow, had stuffed a cherry into his gun. The minister, feeling something strike his chest, looked down and saw a widening spot of crimson. Clutching his chest and speaking in an agonized tone audible to the very back of the audience, he exclaimed, "My God, I AM shot!"

I forget why McCracken told the story—I think it was to illustrate the meaning of existentialism—but it is easy to imagine that the young minister in the Scottish kirk was instantly loved and feted by his parishioners as a really good sport. He became one of them a lot faster than if he had not relented and played the part in their play.

73

Don't ever tell stories on your parishioners unless you have first asked their permission.

Even then, you should never tell a story that puts a parishioner in a negative light. Only tell stories that make them look good or human or funny.

One minister I knew in Nashville told a rather long, involved story about a woman who had belonged to a former parish of his in Florida. He didn't use her name, but the story left a negative impression of the woman as a person, who had lied and taken advantage of others. After the service, a visitor passing through the reception line said, "You were talking about Marge So-and-So in Fort Lauderdale, weren't you?" Startled and trapped, the minister blinked and nodded his head. Afterward, he told me how terrible he felt.

"I never imagined," he said, "that anybody a thousand miles away would be in the congregation and hear me tell that story about Marge. I felt awful!"

That's always a risk we run, however, when we tell any story about a person we've known. So it's best to live by two rules: first, don't ever tell a negative story about anybody you've known, and, second, get permission even when you want to tell a positive story.

The downside of telling stories about anybody you know is that people who come to you for counseling will begin to worry that you might someday reveal something about them in a sermon. They may become reticent to talk about any sensitive matters in their lives, for fear that what they say will return to haunt them.

Most people of whom you ask permission to share a good story will readily grant it, although they may say, "Leave my name out of it, if you don't mind. I'd just as soon not have the publicity."

And this word of warning about publishing sermons with people's stories in them: ministers have been sued for revealing things in print even after the persons involved didn't object to having their stories used in the context of a Sunday worship service.

74

Take an occasional sabbatical from your ministry.

You need some leave from time to time, a chance to withdraw from the give-and-take of your busy life and deal with all the questions and ideas that have arisen in the course of it. I have never known either a minister or a teacher who went away for a minimum of three months or a maximum of twelve without coming back refreshed, recharged, and ready to fight with a pack of wolves!

In case you aren't aware of it, the Lilly Foundation's religion department has been providing funding for ministers' sabbatical leaves for several years now, and is very proud of the results of their munificence. Their contract for a sabbatical leave is always with the individual minister's church, not with the minister him or herself. They provide funding for the church to hire a substitute for the pastor while the pastor is away, and to give the minister a very livable wage during the interim. Sometimes the foundation even provides travel money if the pastor wants to go to some other place to do research, investigate another ministry, or merely widen his or her view of things by seeing other places.

One minister from Wisconsin, Rev. Lawrence Balleine, used his Lilly grant a few years ago to create a special Lenten diary. Leaving on U.S. Route 41 at its northernmost point, where it extends into a small peninsula on Lake Michigan, he followed it all the way down to where it ends at the ocean in Miami, Florida. In the forty days that he invested in the trip, Balleine visited interesting points, often of religious significance, along the way, and developed a meditation around each stop. One was at a Native American festival in Tennessee. Another was at President Jimmy Carter's church in Plains, Georgia, where he met President Carter and attended the Sunday school class the former president teaches. During the year after he made this interesting trip, Balleine edited and published his diary, and it was used by his parishioners as a basis of Lenten meditation the following spring.

Other ministers have used their sabbatical leaves to attend special classes in Oxford University or the University of Edinburgh; visit the worshiping community in Taize, France; do research in several churches across the United States on matters of spirituality, finance, church growth, and other subjects; and stay at home to write poetry or fiction embodying insights from their pastoral backgrounds.

75

Be aware of the power of sexual attraction between you and certain people you meet as a minister.

It is hard to pick up a major newspaper or journal without reading a story about some pastor who has gotten in trouble for having sexual relations with someone they were counseling.

It isn't any wonder. We are sexual machines, in a way; our bodies are constituted in such a way that they are easily attracted to certain members of the opposite sex (or, in the case of homosexuals, certain members of the same sex). Nature planned it this way for the propagation of the species. The only difference between us and animals in the barnyard is that we have had the advantage of training to understand the advantages, both spiritual and practical, of being monogamous.

But people who live in the public eye are often vulnerable to their own magnetism for those who see them there. Pastors, like politicians, movie stars, stage actors, and television personalities, often look especially good to others because they are so visible. Henry Kissinger, the physically unattractive Secretary of State under President Richard Nixon, was often seen with attractive women. "They are attracted to the smell of power," he said on one occasion. "I can't help it, but I can enjoy it."

This attraction poses special difficulties for ministers, who live in a fishbowl and are supposed to be paragons of moral virtue. When they slip and fall, even for a brief time, somebody usually finds out and it means the end of their ministry. I know several fine ministers, among the country's best and brightest, who have had to leave the Christian ministry because they were unfaithful to their mates.

These days, ministers sometimes get into trouble by joining improper chat rooms on the Internet or becoming involved in long, intimate e-mail affairs. I have mentioned one young man I knew who had an outstanding career in a Southern church until he became so exhausted in his work that he began several ongoing chat-room relationships and ended up being unfaithful to his wife. Fortunately, after a divorce and years of counseling, he and his wife were rejoined in marriage and the family was brought together again. But it isn't always that way.

Guard against a spirit of lust. Let others know how committed you are to your mate and your home. Never counsel a person of the opposite sex in a place where you cannot be viewed through a glass or a partially open door. Conduct yourself with faultless propriety. Avoid doing or saying anything that could be construed as morally compromising. You have everything to lose!

76

Remember the power of the Holy Spirit.

No minister ought to need reminding of this, but most of us forget it, especially in the most pressing times of our ministries.

I remember a story Lawrence LeShan once told about this wonderful power. He said that when he was a boy riding somewhere with his father, they came upon the scene of an accident. A man who was changing a tire had been hurt when the car fell off its jack, and was lying beneath the frame of the car. LeShan's father, a strong man, bent his back and leaned against the car. He told his son, "Larry, you pull him out when I lift the car." Then he heaved himself against the automobile, lifting it off the injured man. LeShan never forgot this remarkable demonstration of what one person can do in a time of crisis.

That's the way it is when we call on the Holy Spirit, he said; we are empowered to do things we normally could not do.

It's true.

No one I've ever known lived constantly in the power of the Spirit. But I have known many Christians who did remarkable things at specific times when they called on this power and let it inhabit their lives. They didn't look any different on the outside, but something happened inside them. It was as if they suddenly became like those energized comic-book heroes, capable of doing incredible things.

I have often seen it happen in a fellowship of Christian people—something extraordinary fills the air and their wills yield to a higher power than their own. But it sometimes happens in the lives of individuals as well, and pastors are missing the best part of their own capabilities if they aren't living close enough to the Spirit of God to call on that Spirit from time to time to make a difference in something important, such as the healing of a parishioner, the solving of a personal problem, or the mending of a broken or angry heart.

Most ministers use the words "in the name of the Father, Son, and Holy Spirit" a dozen times a week. But how often do we stop to think about the availability of the Spirit in our lives to transform them from the weak, ordinary lives they are into vessels of power for God?

Sadly, we are often like electric cords lying beside a plug containing a power connection that can send incredible energy through them but that never get plugged in. Don't forget, in your ministry, where the real power is!

Respect everybody's theology, regardless of how far it is from your own.

Admittedly, this isn't always easy. It can be very difficult to listen to some people's harebrained ideas about heaven and hell, the end of the world, the pathway to God, and other hot-button theological issues without wondering if they were behind the door when the smarts were being passed out.

But when you think how silly your own notions and understanding can appear to someone else—say, a world-class theologian or a Nobel Prize-winning scientist—it may give you a little more patience for the person you think is a religious buffoon.

Someone once described our knowledge of the universe as being similar to that of a goldfish that swims around in its bowl all day and imagines it understands the lives of the human beings it sees peering in at it or putting food in its water from time to time. Actually, most of us have seen a lot less meaningfully into eternity and the destiny of the human soul than the goldfish has seen into the nature of human existence.

Given our vast ignorance about most things, then, it is reasonable for us to be tolerant of the viewpoints of others. Even though they may appear ridiculous or less than sophisticated to us, they may look almost as good as ours in the eyes of God.

Disagreeing about theology may produce friction between us and some of the people we know. One thing we can be certain of, though, is that love and relationship are more important than philosophical or religious differences. Almost all great spiritual leaders assure us that love is the final goal of all religions. So let's keep that in mind whenever we are tempted to ridicule the theological opinions of others.

78

Resist the temptation to use your position as a minister to gain special favors of any kind.

Being clergy is important. Of course it is. But it doesn't entitle you to break line at the cafeteria or get out of a speeding ticket. If you ever try to use it that way, you will be disgracing your calling.

I remember Brother Raymond Aubrey. Raymond was an old-fashioned Baptist minister I knew when I was a student in graduate school. He hadn't been to college, so he spent his life ministering in small, rural churches while holding down a regular job as an accountant. He had a big heart and a strong sense of humor, and I enjoyed being around him.

One time I saw him so angry he could have bitten a ten-penny nail in two.

"What's the matter, Raymond?" I asked.

"That gol-darned guy at the store down by my church," he said enigmatically.

I waited for an explanation. He looked at me and realized I was waiting, so he went on with it.

"Tried to give me a pair of socks," he said. "I went in his store to visit him. He's a mean-spirited ol' coot most of the time, and I don't like him. But today he tried to give me a pair of socks."

"So?" I said.

"I told him that if the church of which he is a deacon would pay me enough, I could buy my own socks! I refused to take them."

Raymond had a point. He wasn't in Christ's ministry to get special favors from people. He didn't need a discount on what he bought. He wouldn't have gone to the head of the line or taken free tickets to a movie because he was a minister. And he certainly didn't want to be beholden to that storeowner for a pair of socks.

I think I might have figured out a way to take the socks and be gracious to the man who wanted me to have them, but I respect Raymond's stand and think we need to remember that we're not in the ministry in order to profit from it. We're in the ministry to serve God, and we should never intend to get an advantage from others because we're privileged to have a calling.

79

Bring in qualified consultants to study your church and its ministries.

Consultants are rarely better than the information provided to them by the officials of your church, but, given as much accurate information as possible, they can bring a great deal to your people's vision of themselves and what they are or are not achieving in the work of the kingdom of God. Sure, they're expensive. But which of us doesn't want to consult a good diagnostician occasionally for a medical situation or even a tune-up on the car?

Make it a big affair for the congregation. Involve them in the review. Celebrate the occasion with a dinner—many dinners, even. Don't sit tightly on any reports. Make them public—the more public, the better. Discuss them openly. Pray about them. Gather the congregation around them and make decisions about where the church should go next.

What are you likely to find? Any number of things are possible. That you have too few or too many staff members. That you aren't using volunteers properly. That you project the wrong image to visitors. That you are neglecting ministries to the poor and homeless. That your youth group is idling when it ought to be zooming. That you have a poor self-concept as a church and need to see yourselves in a different light. Any number of things, any one of which could be well worth the cost of the consultations.

You don't have to buy everything consultants say. But their word ought to be important to you if you have looked around and brought in highly recommended consultants. It ought to cause you to rethink a lot of things you're doing or not doing. It will leave you with a much clearer self-image and some specific goals you want to meet.

"Golly," said one pastor, whose church had just gone through such a guided self-study, "we had no idea we were doing such a good job in some areas and such a poor one in others. We've got a lot to do!"

80

Have an office that says "welcome" to all visitors.

Ambience counts for a lot in almost any business, but nowhere more than in the office of a pastor. People who come to see you will take unconscious clues from the way your office looks. If it is cluttered and junky, they will feel superfluous in it, and possibly nervous to get away. If it is stark and ascetic, some people—notably engineers and mathematicians—will feel okay about it, while others may feel anxious and on display. If it is warm and cozy, with appropriate furnishings and perhaps soft music, almost everyone will feel comfortable there—even you.

Think about how nice it is simply to have an office. I served a few small churches where there wasn't one, and if someone wanted to see me, they either had to come to the parsonage for a visit or meet sitting side by side on a pew. Ever since, having a nicely appointed office has been a blessing to me, and I have cherished being able to visit with folks in a welcoming environment.

Give some real thought to what you would like your office to say to people. Do you have a lot of important books there, so they will be impressed by your knowledge and acquaintance with the great classics of the faith? How about photos that say, *I'm a family man and these are my pride and joy*? Or perhaps documents that tell where you've been, such as diplomas, certificates from pastoral-care programs, or plaques awarded for meritorious service?

I think I always wanted my office to say, to whoever came to see me, "I'm so glad you're here and we can have this visit." That's why the colors are muted and warm, the furniture is comfortable, and the decorations are pleasant and artistic. I want you to be able to relax here and tell me your innermost hopes and fears. I invite you to speak of your secret desires and anxieties. Together, in this quiet and lovely place, we shall join our spirits in the Lord, and you will go away more confident about your life and what you should be doing with it.

81

Maintain a store of special books, CDs, and DVDs you can give or loan to people who need them.

For a while, when I was a minister at Marble Collegiate Church in New York, I used the office that had formerly belonged to Dr. Florence Pert, who was more responsible than anyone else for designing and implementing the programs of that famous old church. Florence, in her earlier career, had been very active in Faith at Work, and she and her husband, George, had traveled all over the United States and abroad, conducting and attending programs for that formidable organization. Because she had been so heavily involved in Faith at Work and its literature, her bookshelves, which I inherited, were filled with duplicate copies of books by many of the great Christian leaders of our time: Bruce Larson, Keith Miller, Paula D'Arcy, Sam Shoemaker, and, of course, Norman Vincent Peale.

I often imagined Florence in her heyday talking with people in that office and then handing them a book before they left, saying, "Here, take this and read it sometime. I think it will find a sweet spot in your mind and heart because of some of the things we've been discussing." It was her way of prolonging a conference and extending her ministry into other people's lives.

Make the purchase of these materials part of your pastoral allowance. Or if the church can't afford it, maybe they could be a part of your own stewardship, your gift to the church and the people to whom you minister.

Pore over the various religious catalogs for things you think would be useful to people—books and CDs for young people, young marrieds, people feeling a call to special service, people in mid-life crisis, people thinking about retiring, those with the problems of their elder years. Be sure to read the books and listen to the CDs yourself, so you don't give things to people that might prove inappropriate or even useless.

As someone once said to me about Florence Pert, "I rarely went to see her about anything that I didn't come away with at least two books she was eager for me to read. And once in a while, one of those books would change my life!"

82

Bless the beasts (and children).

Think how many households in your parish have at least a dog or cat, not to mention hamsters, guppies, snakes, and parakeets. And people love their pets. You may even be called upon occasionally, as I have been, to conduct a funeral service for one.

If you want to do something very popular, have a blessing service for animals on St. Francis's birthday or a Sunday near it. You'll be surprised by how many people will show up, including your devoted parishioners, but also a lot of people they know. You may also be surprised at the kinds of animals that will appear on the church lawn—horses, ponies, monkeys, tropical fish, maybe even a jackass or two.

Read texts that indicate the connection between human beings and their animals—the Genesis account of creation, the woman who told Jesus that even the little dogs could eat the crumbs from the children's table, Balaam's ass, Zechariah's account of the Messiah arriving on the back of a foal, Jesus' entry into Jerusalem, maybe even the Four Horsemen of the Apocalypse. Give a brief talk on animals, maybe even pointing out that some people have theorized that there will be animals in heaven (e.g., Harry Butman's *Brown Boy* [Padre Productions, 1989], about his favorite cat), and have a prayer for the health and well-being of all the animals present.

Be sure to have some photographers there to take pictures for those who want them (you'll be popular with the paparazzi, especially if you're in a robe and stole), and maybe somebody from the local paper. It never hurts to get a little free publicity for the church, especially when the people it attracts are those who love animals.

83

Work at finding new ways your church can serve the poor in your area.

A lot of people admit that they don't actually know poor people. It isn't that they've tried to avoid them or don't like them, only that they aren't thrown in with them very naturally or don't live next door to them. They sincerely want to help the poor. They can't read the Gospel of Luke or hear sermons about love and service without occasionally feeling twinges of longing to really do something for those who don't have the advantages they have. So many of them will welcome new, innovative programs for helping the poorer people around the community.

One way is to have a food warehouse and provide food for the various agencies that serve the poor. It takes space, somebody with a truck, and some volunteers to canvas restaurants and markets for donated products.

Another way is to have a soup kitchen on certain days a week. In some communities, the churches take turns, one doing it on Monday, another on Tuesday, and so on. Others have food closets where food gifts are stored for needy people. Still others have arrangements with certain merchants that they can send people to them with coupons for special packages of food.

Some churches provide sleeping space for the homeless, and volunteers take turns spending the night at the church to look after these people. Sometimes movies are shown before lights out, complete with boxes of popcorn, so everyone goes to bed in a good mood.

For many homeless people, one of the most valuable things churches can do is provide bathrooms where they can use the toilets and take showers. Packages of soap, shampoo, toothpaste, toothbrushes, combs, and little make-up kits are sometimes furnished. Most of us have no idea how good a little spritz of cologne or perfume can make a homeless person feel.

At least one church I know has counseling services for people looking for work, a particular boon in these bad economic times when so many people are out of work. Another offers phone service for people to call their relatives in other cities or parts of the country.

Many middle- and upper-class church members often find their lives changed as a result of their working with the poor, and some become dedicated to a lifelong ministry of finding ways to ameliorate the hard times of poor people in a society of wealth. And ministers sometimes find that the same thing happens to them. One minister wrote to me, "I was one of the Christians who blithely thought about eternal salvation and not about the needs of people in the here and now until I led a mission trip to Haiti and saw the extreme poverty in that island. Then I came home and realized there was similar poverty all around me. I haven't been the same since."

84

Develop a matchmaker mentality.

That is, turn yourself into a special one-person agency for putting people together. You are in a unique position to know a lot of people and often to know a great deal about them. Therefore you should begin to see which people ought to know other people you know or be apprised of opportunities from which they could benefit.

You've doubtless heard about the "six degrees of separation" theory, in which it is said that we are all only six people removed from anyone we'd like to meet or anything we'd like to do. The secret is to figure out the connections and how to get from where you presently are to where you'd like to be.

Unfortunately, a lot of people may not be getting connected, even though they live in the same town or attend the same church with someone who could help them.

Think of yourself, then, as the magic-maker, the one who knows enough to start people on their way to success with their lives or their work by introducing them to someone they need to meet.

A lady in your church may make beautiful hats and dream of one day being a great millinery artist. You happen to know a banker who is always looking for a small business to develop for the sake of his own business. So you introduce the two over lunch, and voilà, an important relationship is begun.

Someone in your church writes poetry, but seldom talks about it to anybody but you. You know he'd like to get a volume of his poems published but doesn't know how. You happen to be acquainted with an author who has published several volumes of poetry. So you bring the two of them together so the successful writer can help the less experienced one.

My friend Carrie McIndoe, who was a brilliant financial consultant in Boston, moved to New York to help her sister raise an adopted child from China. She needed a new job, so she applied to the government for a grant to help teenagers learn to be businesspersons, on the theory that this would keep them out of trouble and lower the crime rate. When she received the grant, she began going around the country holding workshops for teenagers to teach them the basics of economics and business practice. At the end of each workshop, she had the participants present plans for new businesses they dreamed of starting. She also brought in local bankers and entrepreneurs to watch, listen, and critique the plans, and encouraged them to "adopt" the young people and guide them through the process of getting started.

How satisfying, you think. Yes, and imagine yourself in that role as a pastor. There are many people in your own parish whom you could help in a similar way. Just become the matchmaker God has put you in the position to be.

85

Accompany your parishioners on pilgrimages.

Seriously. You might be surprised at how close you will become to those church members who take a long trip with you. There is something about going to Europe or the Holy Land or South America with the pastor that creates a bond nothing else can match.

You may not know it, but most tour companies are happy to work with pastors to set up special tours for their congregants. So happy, in fact, that they will send the pastor for free if there are as many as five or six members who agree to take the tour. They'll even send the pastor's spouse or partner for free if there are ten or twelve participants. Beyond that, they might even pay a cash bonus. After all, to them it's a business.

I know one pastor who specializes in taking his elder members on trips. He has been doing it for years, and has visited such exotic places as Nova Scotia, Peru, Italy, the Greek Islands, England, Ireland, and South Africa. "After eight or ten such trips," he says, "I have a real core of loyal supporters in the congregation whom I can always count on to support my programs for the church."

Another pastor has made a specialty of taking his young people on tours. "I really get to know the kids when we get away from this country," he said. "We develop a special bond on foreign soil, and they talk about almost everything you can imagine, especially their parents, their dreams, and their disappointments. I spend my whole trip pastoring, and it's great fun at the same time. We come back as a team, and I can tell a difference in their lives from then on. They're never quite the same standoffish youngsters they were before the trip."

If you really want to use such trips to develop a greater spirituality in your people, design them around special places of religious significance or holiness, such as Canterbury, Lourdes, the Vatican, Taize, Gethsemani Abbey, or a hundred other similar locations that are important in Christian history. Two or three pastors who enjoy musical events participate each year in the Three Choirs Festival, which alternates among three locations in southwest England. Others take groups to important educational centers such as Edinburgh, Cambridge, and Oxford, pointing out the significant historical events that have taken place in those locations. The possibilities are endless.

86

Be generous to your predecessors.

This is difficult for some ministers, who feel threatened every time some parishioner recalls what a loving pastor old Dr. Bartlett had been or how wonderful Rev. Wanamaker was in the pulpit. But for heaven's sake, the ministry is not a competition sport. Jesus put the skids under that idea back when James and John asked for permission to sit at his side in the kingdom and he gave them a little lecture on real discipleship.

You owe a lot to your predecessors. Some of them made it possible for your church to survive and be in a position to pay your salary now. Others developed classes and preached sermons that made some of the fine Christians who are now your best members and leading encouragers.

Your members will appreciate your having a warm appreciation for the ministers who preceded you. Some were baptized by them. Others had their lives transformed by sermons they preached. Still others are grateful for the sheer fact of the continuity they provided for your place of worship and the existence of the congregation itself. Your speaking kindly of those who came before you will make them like you better and make them more happily disposed to the church as a community of saints.

If any of your predecessors live in the community or continue to worship in your church, so much the better. Get to know them, welcome them to everything, and give them things to do. If they are retired, they're probably aching to get back into the ministry, even in small doses. Encourage them to take an occasional wedding or funeral.

Have them teach a class. Invite them to sit with you in the chancel and lead the morning prayer.

Be kind and forgiving if occasionally a former pastor seems to want to upstage or out-brag you. It's a natural fault. Remember that you may be in that position some day yourself. How well you tolerate competition is in large part a measure of your saintliness.

87

Attend the meetings of your elderly church members.

Some churches call them the Over Sixties, Wise Crackers, Keenagers, Golden Agers, or Late Bloomers. It doesn't matter what they're called. They are among the most important charges you have in your parish, and you should spend as much time as possible in their midst.

You'll profit by it. If you're relaxed and not rushing through their lunches or meetings to get to another meeting, you'll hear and learn things that will enrich not only your whole ministry but your personal life as well. Those people are fountains of understanding, and they rarely turn off the water. If you don't come away every time with a few pearls of wisdom, then you are undoubtedly the porcine beast before whom they were reportedly cast.

Not only are the elder citizens of the church the smartest about most things, they're also the most tender and loving. No longer caught up in the busyness that enervates and devalues so many people's lives, they have time to be generously disposed toward everyone. They know how to share themselves and what they have with others. They know how to have fun, and to make their world lighter and brighter in the process. In short, they're in the blessing business.

Be a familiar face around their retirement homes. If you have an hour or two to spare, drive over and walk through the lounge, stopping to visit with whomever you see there. People will get accustomed to your being there and will start looking forward to your visits.

88

Do everything you can to create bridges between your church and local artists.

Artists are, after all, the life's breath of any people. Like God, they're in the business of making.

Through the ages, Christianity has inspired the greatest artists of every nation. There is such a density of great art in a place like Florence, Italy, for example—most of it commissioned by the church or inspired by Christ—that it is known for something called "Stendhal's syndrome." The French writer Stendhal once became ill in Florence; his symptoms included dizziness, fainting, rapid heartbeat, confusion, and possibly hallucinations. When doctors couldn't find any cause, they realized it was his overexcitement about being in such an enriched environment. Now doctors say about 200 people a year come down with Stendhal's syndrome when visiting that richly art-filled city.

Why shouldn't the church be profiting from the talents of artists of every kind today? Painters, sculptors, water colorists, poets, novelists, singers, instrumentalists, photographers, weavers, designers, even macramé makers. Why not have an art fair once a year and encourage people to contribute to it? Or perhaps coordinate art tours to nearby museums and theaters.

Sure, art is "dangerous." Artists are less inhibited than the rest of us because they listen to their inner muses. They often prefer to work at the edge of what is known or understood. Therefore a lot of religious people worry that they'll do something "out of line" or even scandalous, like that photographer who exhibited a picture of a cross floating in a toilet.

Walter Rhodes, a Broadway actor who spent a lot of time working at Asolo Theater in St. Petersburg, once told me, "I don't think art and religion make very compatible bedfellows." It was his reason, he said, for seldom going to church.

But stop for a moment and think about Jesus. He worried the orthodox folks in his day, didn't he? He didn't exactly color inside the lines, or at least not the lines they had set for the people to observe. Can we really follow him by staying inside the lines in our day?

Plymouth Congregational Church in Minneapolis has a 281-seat theater in which it contracts four distinguished new plays to be performed every year. Every theatergoer in Minneapolis and for miles around reveres and respects that church for its active role in the arts.

Many churches have art shows, photography exhibits, furniture fairs, and other ways of honoring their most creative spirits. Why shouldn't we all do that? After all, if it weren't for some pretty fine artists, most of us wouldn't have the beautiful buildings we have, with their graceful furnishings and stained-glass windows.

89

Regularly set aside time to think and recreate your inner self.

Actually, for a minister, this usually qualifies as prayer time. It has to do with backing away from regular duties for a significant block of time—say, two or three hours, at least—and clearing the mind of all the detritus that naturally collects during a busy week, then luxuriating in time to think, imagine, and reposition things.

I am often amazed by how automatic most ministers' lives become after a little while in the parish. They merely do what they have to do, and keep on doing it in the same old way without ever reflecting on whether it's the best way or how their time might be better spent doing something else.

The best ministers I've known take time to ponder. They shut down their engines, quit driving, driving, driving, and drift along in neutral for a while, letting their minds and hearts explore all the myriad possibilities just waiting to be discovered. It is during times like this that their great decisions arise, great sermons are born, and their lives achieve real stature.

Maybe we ought to develop a formula—say, 30/1 or 25/2. That is, for every thirty hours we spend going full throttle through our week, we should resolve to spend at least one hour with the motor shut off. Or for every twenty-five hours, two. You have to decide what you're willing to do.

But think of it this way. Most of us realize we need to go to the gym or the tennis court or the running trail for a certain amount of time each week. Our bodies require it. Why not recognize what our hearts and minds require to stay at their best too?

A wise minister friend once said to me, "I find that I can only do this job well if I put my 'Gone fishing' sign on the door at least once or twice a week and take some time for gestating—just being. If I forget to do that, I'm in trouble, and the next time I remember, I mentally fuss at myself for having forgotten because I know I haven't done my best at all the things I've done."

90

Watch your volunteers to see which ones ought to be elevated to staff positions.

This is one of the best ways to find good staff members.

Everybody knows what a grab bag it is when you advertise for somebody to be a youth leader or work with the elderly or manage weddings. There's an interview process, heads are scratched, and then half-hearted decisions are reached. And then there's the waiting to see how they worked out, and the worry, in some cases, of having to draw them aside and say, "I'm sorry, but . . . ."

It's much more efficient just to keep a close eye on the people who take on jobs voluntarily and then turn out to be very good at them. Some great churches do almost all their staffing this way.

Ernest Campbell, the pastor at Riverside Church in New York a few years ago, told me that he got a crackerjack Christian education person this way. He did the interview gig, he said, but wasn't happy with the people it turned up. Then he sat back and watched what one of the lay volunteers was doing with the parts of the program she worked on and was pleased at what he saw. So he asked her one day if she would like to do the job full time and for pay.

"She turned out to be the best Christian ed leader I ever had," he said. "She's a jewel!"

91

Have a good long-range planning committee and keep them working diligently.

It has been many years now since Alvin Toffler's *Future Shock* appeared (Random House, 1970), reminding us of what we were already discovering, that everything happens so rapidly in our culture today that we haven't recovered from one tsunami before we're hit by another. If anything, the pace has only accelerated. Consider the commercial lifespan of the average cell phone or computer. What is it now, about six months? Some of us are so far behind the curve on everything that we expect to meet ourselves coming back around before long.

No church can afford not to think about its future ministry in times like these. As technology enables us to do more and more outreach—Does your church blog? Does it webcast?—we need to have well-chosen long-range planning committees at work over the crystal ball. Otherwise, the future will overwhelm us and be gone before we know we've had it.

Such committees need a variety of individuals—financiers, architects, electronic experts, psychologists, educators, and computer nerds, to name a few—and should meet regularly to discuss really important agendas, not merely to satisfy our need to say we're looking at the church's future.

Think of it as stewardship. God has entrusted a churchful of people into our hands. We have five and ten years ahead to think about, not merely now and the problems that are on our plate today. We should be anticipating what our needs and problems will look like in ten years, as well as the new opportunities that may be open to us. Such crystal-ball gazing can be extremely important in rapidly changing times.

One church I know listened to its long-range planning committee when the committee studied the shifting real estate patterns of its community and decided that the church should actually change its location in order to take advantage of the changing patterns. Many parishioners objected that it was foolish to undergo a relocation, mostly because they were comfortable where they were. But a few years later everybody was glad they did change, because their old church was left behind in what became largely a warehouse area, while their new one was in the center of an energetic area of family growth.

92

Run your own referral agency.

Just kidding, of course. Well, not quite. Every pastor ought to develop a highly accurate and efficient listing of people to whom parishioners can be directed for various needs, including doctors, therapists, psychologists, psychiatrists, family counselors, a good Alcoholics Anonymous center, an Al-Anon group, an Alzheimer's support group, an ongoing grief group, a sexual-addiction group, a drug-counseling program, and other help agents and agencies as needed.

Many pastors are lazy about this and wait until faced with a parish emergency before making inquiries about good referrals. The lag time may be critical, so those lists ought to be in place not long after a pastor arrives on the scene.

It's also easier to compile such a list when there is no particular pressure on you to locate a certain kind of helper. You can make a point of discussing potential future needs with various local authorities—medical, legal, social, and so on—and following up, where possible, with actual meetings with the people you might be recommending.

In an interview with, say, a child psychologist, you can ascertain what the professional's training is, whether they are familiar with your congregation or any of its members, what their fee or insurance arrangements are, and what kind of religious views they may hold. You can actually create a file on each person, with notes that will remind you of critical things you want to remember if confronted with the need for the person.

Then, when someone comes to you as the pastor and has a particular kind of problem you think you need help with, you can say, "Do you happen to know Dr. So-and-So, the psychiatrist? She specializes in working with elderly patients, and I think she would be terrific to meet with your dad and help him adjust to this problem he's having. Could I phone her for you?"

Don't stop with the initial file you've created. Follow up with people you've referred to the experts and see how they felt after their meetings. Jot down notes about their feelings and opinions so you'll have an even better file than before.

Who knows? Your intelligent approach to the referral aspects of your calling may impress some of the experts so much that they'll come to investigate your services and find out for themselves what it might be like to belong to your church family.

93

Craft some really good prayers and liturgical formats for the sacraments of baptism, the Lord's Supper, marriage, and burial.

If you're not creative, at least find some well-written services others have written, do a little altering to suit your own situation, and adopt them for your own use. These are special moments for your congregation that deserve the most thoughtful and meaningful words you can give them.

If your church baptizes infants, think about things that will enhance the moment for the parents, godparents, and other worshipers. I always found it was good to walk each child up the aisle (usually in my arms) and let the people in the back pews see what those up front have already seen; that is, how beautiful a child is at his or her baptism. Make your prayers for the children and parents particularly appropriate and memorable. Give the parents copies so they can keep them in the children's scrapbooks. They may mean a lot to some of them years later.

Develop a style for serving Communion that dignifies the service but is also comfortable to you. Make it both homely and eloquent. Cultivate silences as well as sound. Let it be an unusually high moment in the life of your congregation, so that all who participate have a sense of having been with God.

As for weddings and funerals or memorial services, I have said before that these should be highly personalized to relate to the ones upon whom they focus. Think about each occasion. Don't merely "turn out another one." Let each be a totally thoughtful and meaning-ful event.

One thing to remember about baptisms, weddings, and funerals is that there will often be guests in your midst who aren't members of your congregation. Let them feel how special it is to be part of your fellowship. They might even decide to worship with you on a regular basis.

94

Listen—really listen— to your fellow staff members.

That means the secretaries as well as other ministers and programmers. You aren't the only one with good ideas. They may surprise you by how helpful they can be with ideas and suggestions.

I have known pastors who liked to speed through weekly staff get-togethers as if they were rushing through a stoplight before it turned red. They would have been happy to conduct the meetings without anyone else there, because they could have finished sooner and been off to other things.

But a staff meeting is a great boon to the pastor. It is a privilege to have everybody assembled away from the phones (provided, of course, you ban cell phones during meetings), relaxed, munching on brownies or coffee cake, sipping a hot drink, and tuned into groupthink. Wonderful things can happen during this time.

Think of yourself as a kind of group leader, poised at the board with your magic marker to jot down suggestions. Be a conduit, a vehicle, a stimulator. Turn what could have been a deadly, dull session into one that's alert, alive, and full of vibrations.

Your staff members will love you for this, and you will come away armed with all kinds of ideas and suggestions you probably wouldn't have come up with alone.

95

Subscribe to some really worthwhile print or online magazines and pore through them during your spare moments at home or in the office.

As a matter of fact, it's probably better to receive some at one place and the rest at the other.

You need to read at least one of the top weekly news magazines, such as *Time, Newsweek,* or *U.S. News & World Report.* Read them for the main news stories so you'll be up on what's happening in the world. The "Religion" section is sometimes interesting, but usually not as germane as what you'll get from *Christianity Today, The Christian Century,* and *Sojourners,* which you should also read.

Many pastors find *Reader's Digest* a helpful magazine because it has so many human-interest stories. Somebody could actually compile a book of sermon illustrations from old issues of this journal. But the essays are often meaningful too. And you could do worse than imitate the *Reader's Digest* style in your own writing, because it is always crystal clear and eminently readable. Remember that Benjamin Franklin learned his limpid prose style by copying out essays from *The Spectator* and *The Tatler,* high-class journals by English writers Addison and

Steele. So don't be shy about imitating the really good use of language found in *Reader's Digest*.

Scan the magazine racks at a good bookstore to see which other magazines you might find interesting and informative. *Smithsonian*, for example, is always attractively composed and filled with fine articles. The same can be said for *National Geographic*, *Atlantic*, and *Harper's*.

Most of the big-name newspapers can now be read online, and if you're the minister of a large church, filled with attorneys, doctors, and financiers, among others, you might want to check *The New York Times*, *The Washington Post*, and *The Wall Street Journal* on a regular basis.

While you don't want to be a name-dropper in your sermons, it doesn't hurt, once in a while, to allude to a fine journal or newspaper that some of your members are bound to read.

96

Pastor your deacons.

They are your first line of contact with the membership, and whatever you invest in them at a pastoral level will filter out to many others in the congregation.

Earlier, I said you should work the margins of your congregation and not worry about those at the center. But the diaconate is an exception, if for no other reason than the one I have just given. These are the men and women who will carry your ideas, your theology, and your concerns to the rest of your people.

Think of them as your disciples, the way Christ had disciples. He spent far more time with Peter, James, John, and the others than with the crowds of nameless people of whom we catch only glimpses in the Gospels. It was they, when he had gone, who translated his teachings and will into the practical form of the church. And, similarly, your deacons will do more than anyone else to affect the rank-and-file members of your congregation.

Consider how you can best lead your deacons over the entire tenure of your pastorate. Perhaps you will wish to hold an annual or semi-annual retreat for them in which you can talk about many things, the way Jesus probably did when he took his disciples away from the crowds. You may decide to give an important little devotional lesson at each deacons' meeting, or even teach a mini-lesson on certain aspects of ecclesiology. Or you may want to import some talent for periodic deacons' meetings—such as an expert in pastoral care or a long-term planning expert—and let these persons share their insights and inspiration with your officers.

In most churches, the deacons' first lines of responsibility include the pastoral care of the congregation and leadership in weekly worship. You could consider offering a course in hospital visitation or some other subject that would enhance the personal ministries of the deacons. You might even give them basic lessons in the history and meaning of worship.

Make it your goal to get to know your deacons as intimately as possible, learning about their life histories, their present situations, and their dreams and aspirations. If you are able to be their pastor and create a pastoral bond with them, you will not have any real trouble pastoring the rest of your church.

97

Make a point of getting to know and being kind to your ushers.

Of course you want to know and be kind to everyone. But consider the ushers and how vital they are. They are the very first line of connection between your church and visitors, as well as agents of comfort and welcome to your members. The first impression registered in the visitors' minds, apart from how lovely and welcoming the building itself is, will probably be made by these unique people.

Maximilian, the holy Roman emperor, said he always placed his finest soldiers in the phalanx, where the enemy would meet them ahead of all his armies, because he wished to terrify the opposition with their fearsome gallantry.

In a way, that's what you're doing, strategically speaking, by befriending and working with your ushers.

It's very important for the ushers to be "high" on their pastor, so that they will assure visitors, "You'll really like our minister. She (or he) is a fine person and an unusually good preacher." And as the visitors leave, expressing thanks and their high regard for you, they can clinch the matter by responding, "Oh, yes, we're very fond of Rev. So-and-So. There isn't a better minister anywhere!"

I don't mean to sound too crassly promotional. What is really at stake between you and the ushers is more profound than that. It has to do with your genuine care for the people who volunteer and make things work around your church, and the importance of taking the

time and effort to make them feel good about being there and working with you. But it doesn't hurt to win some bonus points while
you're about it, does it?

I give wonderfully high marks to the ushers I came to know at
Marble Collegiate Church in New York. There were three primary
entrances to the sanctuary of that lovely church, and I enjoyed seeing
the ushers at each of them. One was a dear little lady named Dorothy
who could make even the Abominable Snowman feel welcome in
church. Another was a tall, handsome gentleman named Phil, who
was a security expert yet had the manners and demeanor of a great
English butler. There was a handsome young couple, Urs and Lori.
Urs was in the banking business, and Lori worked for a company that
serviced large newspapers and other businesses. And there was
Stephen, the nattiest dresser I ever saw, in or out of church, who was
always smiling and as upbeat as a Sousa march.

Nobody came into Marble Church without passing through the
warm bath of attention from these beautiful people. Even if it was a
gray Sunday and the service wasn't quite up to par—which sometimes
happens, even in a great church—the guests and members alike were
all tuned up for worship by the time they had been seated in a pew.

This didn't just happen. One of the staff members, a lovely
woman named Marian Patterson, was in charge of the ushers. She
trained and worked with them and was there every Sunday to field any
questions and solve any problems. They all worked together as harmoniously as if they had been members of the New York Philharmonic
Orchestra on an outing.

I can hear God now, saying to each of them, "Well done, good
and faithful servant."

98

Be careful not to pull the rug out from under your parishioners without warning.

Church people are like all other people: they don't like change. It upsets them to have a minister come in and start moving the pulpit furniture or tampering with the order of the liturgy. So take it easy, parson. Put yourself in their place and ask yourself before you take any drastic action to transform your new parish, *Is this really necessary?*, and if it is, *What should I do to prepare my people for the change?*

There are things you will wish to change, and there are things that ought to be changed. But you can easily defeat your purpose and handicap your ministry by working too quickly and peremptorily to effect change. Learn to count to ten—ten weeks, ten months—before making the move you want to make. Talk to some of your wiser parishioners about the things you're considering, and really listen to their advice. Remember that being your people's pastor and helping them to grow in Christ is more important than the superficial changes you might accomplish by behaving like a bull in a china shop!

I always found that it was a good idea to have a public discussion for any really big issues that needed addressing in the church and then letting people vote on them. Sometimes, in the course of a discussion, I actually changed my mind and voted with the people who opposed my original position. The church is, after all, the original democratic institution in the world, and for the pastor to behave tyrannically or despotically isn't exactly right.

And it's a good idea, even when change has been agreed upon, to be charitable to those who have a hard time with transitions, and make the alterations as gradually as possible. Give everybody breathing time, and walk them through the changes the way you'd walk your own mother through them!

99

Don't be afraid to let your parishioners see you in an apron.

Seriously. Whether you're a man or a woman. Give them the chance to see their pastor at work. Really at work, not just that "mind stuff" you do most of the time.

There are plenty of opportunities if you'll only take them. Such as at church suppers. Or youth group parties. Or clean-up day around the property.

The truth is, people like to see their minister in a humble role occasionally. It means something to them to learn that the pastor actually does menial tasks. Not like one pastor friend of mine, whose personnel board cut out the custodial service because the church could no longer afford it and asked him to take over cleaning the restrooms and sweeping the walks, but in an occasional, good-natured way, helping out with the small things around the church.

Years ago, when I pastored a church a few miles above Boston, we had bean suppers every Saturday night to help meet the budget. The women usually prepared the food and the men did the cleaning up. I took a lot of ribbing from some of the men when I showed up in a frilly apron, but I found that it soon endeared me to them in ways I could never have achieved by my sermons. We did a lot of joking around in the kitchen.

One wag told me to get out of the kitchen because it cramped his style. When I asked how, he said, "Well, I don't feel comfortable saying 'hell' or 'damn' when my minister is in here."

"Is that right?" I asked.

"Yeah," he said, "so get the hell outta here, and don't slam the damn door as you go out!"

This kind of camaraderie is priceless to ministers who often feel that they are working a few feet above the congregation's heads—and actually are, if the chancel is a high one.

100

Remember that your ministry is all about "good news," so try to make people think good news when they come to church, not donuts and downers.

I've visited a lot of churches where the sermon never came near the "good news" center, and the atmosphere of the whole service was, in fact, dolorous and boring. That's a shame, when you think about it, because Christianity was never meant to be sad and pedestrian. In the beginning it was so upbeat that nobody could keep a lid on it. And whenever people have realized their freedom and forgiveness in Christ, there has been a buoyant quality about their worship. So any church that seems tepid and lackluster is plainly missing the mark.

No one in the whole church is more responsible for the attitude in a worship service or any other public meeting than the pastor. If you are up, the congregation will eventually be up; if you're down, they will be down. So always begin, if you intend to be critical of your people and their tone of life, with yourself. Are you happy and eager to serve the Lord? Is everything in order in your own life, so that you transmit a sense of well-being to others? If the answer to either of these questions is no, then you have some serious soul-searching to do. God needs to put you in a blender and shake you up.

Reflect on your prayers and sermons from the last two or three services. Do they adequately reveal the sense of joy and exhilaration that ought to arise from the good news at the heart of the Christian ministry? If not, think about why they don't. Maybe you haven't been conscious enough of the need to install them at the center of what you do, so that their radiance is felt everywhere. Maybe you personally haven't been happy in the Lord of late and need to do some serious praying and recommitting of your life to God.

"What I like about going to church," one woman told me recently, "is the way I come out feeling better and happier than when I went in. I don't know why that is unless it's because the pastor is such a great preacher and I always hear the word of God when I go. I can't miss church. If I do, my whole week is off. It's that simple. My pastor reminds me all the time of what God is doing in my life, and that makes me want to sing!"

101

Be thankful that you serve the greatest calling in the world!

That's true, isn't it? Bar none, it's the greatest! I've never met a good minister who was doing a fine job who wouldn't attest to that.

Most of us forget to be thankful. We allow our attention to be distracted by the little things that hamper or annoy us—people gossiping, others complaining about what we're doing or not doing, some clinging to the past and refusing to go forward, and all the other thorns in a minister's side—and then we become negative and doubting instead of positive and joyous.

Brother David Steindl-Rast, a Benedictine, says in his book *Gratefulness, the Heart of Prayer* (Paulist Press, 1990) that being thankful is the most important part of any Christian's life. He's right about that, isn't he? If our salvation is about anything, it's about being rescued from a humdrum life of blindness and insensitivity so that we see how wonderful all God's gifts and opportunities are and go through life in a spirit of vibrant gratitude.

Who ought to be more thankful about life and its incredible richness than a minister? Who else has the vantage point we share, or a keener sense of God's overwhelming goodness all the time? We aren't just saved to new life, we have been given the key to the storeroom so we can pass out good things to others and make them aware of God's incredible munificence.

Sure, we have our problems. But our calling isn't one of them. Our calling is the most revered in the world. It relates us to God in a way that helps others find God for themselves. It sets us apart, however plain and ordinary we are, as the servants of the Most High. What could be loftier than that? What should give us more constant pleasure?

"We have this ministry," said Paul (2 Cor 4:1). Fact. God has given it to us. God has chosen us out of all the others. God has entrusted us with the news of a kingdom beyond all earthly kingdoms. God has laid a hand on our lives, and others have followed suit and laid their hands on us too.

What more needs to be said? We have only to bow our heads and give thanks. No language can convey our special privilege. It is too high and too deep for words!

Ten Tips Each from Other Ministers: Advice from Those Who Have Been There

From Rev. Jeff Baynes, pastor of Christ United Methodist Church, Albertville, Alabama:

1. Think of ministry, like life itself, as a journey that is living, breathing, and always dynamic.

2. Serve God with your whole heart and don't worry too much about where that will lead you.

3. Be a real shepherd to your flock, always remembering that a lot of them are hurting and that you are supposed to feed and care for them.

4. Inasmuch as many churchgoers don't know the first thing about what it means to be Christians, teach the fundamentals. Christianity 101. Then 102, and so on.

5. Don't ever cheat on your spouse, even in your heart.

6. Don't expect your children to be model preacher's kids; just help them to grow up to be gracious, wholesome human beings.

7. Don't sacrifice your role as a leader of worship to become a mere entertainer.

8. Study your congregation to see who the natural leaders are in their clubs, schools, and community, and work them into leadership roles in the church.

9. Inasmuch as you can't please everyone, don't waste a lot of time trying; instead, guard your core beliefs, your intellect, and your decent humanity, and be as faithful to God as you can.

10. Don't expect to save the world. That's God's function. Your role is to reflect God's plan for divine creation in your ministry.

From Rev. Dr. Amy Butler, senior minister of Calvary Baptist Church, Washington, D.C.:

1. Surround yourself with people who tell you the truth.

2. Remember that it's not about you. Really, it's not.

3. Study and sermon preparation are a discipline; don't let them slide.

4. Your family is not employed by the church.

5. Do everything you can to build and nurture a healthy church staff.

6. Don't take yourself too seriously.

7. Learn how to listen and then do it: listen to people you trust, listen to your church, listen to God, and listen to your gut.

8. Find your community *outside* the church.

9. Give your time and attention to the people who bring life and energy to the church, not the ones who suck it out.

10. Most of all, be a disciple yourself.

From Rev. Dr. Lillian Daniel, senior minister of First Congregational Church (UCC), Glen Ellyn, Illinois:

1. Share stories about yourself in the sermon, not to impress but to make a connection with your hearers. Don't share the kind of stories that will leave people weeping and wondering, "Is the pastor going to be okay?"

2. Dress every day as though you might be called unexpectedly to the hospital or the funeral home. If you don't, you'll be called to come in a hurry on the one day you sneak into the office in your sweatpants.

3. Visit the homes of your parishioners in their normal, more chaotic times. Don't wait to be called for special occasions or times of crisis. Go when the dirty dishes are still in the sink.

4. Don't ever make a point of informing your members about the time you take off for your own needs. Just do it, without making an issue of it.

5. Don't ask permission now for things you don't want to be asking permission for five or ten years from now.

6. Resist the temptation to go back to school too early. In our early years of ministry, we tend to wonder about the knowledge we're missing by not going back. But knowledge comes through experience on the job, too.

7. Resist the temptation to quit. Too many pastors quit before the fun starts.

8. Break bread with your peers. Have lunch every month with other ministers who are at about the same point in ministry as you. If one of them leaves, don't be hasty to find a replacement. Instead, call that person every month and visit by phone. Twenty years from now, your first friends in ministry may be your most important ones.

9. Don't ever refer to your congregation as "they." As the body of Christ, you are now a "we."

10. Remember what your congregation is most worried about when it comes to their new pastor: does she really care about me? New clergy often strive to impress people with what they can do. But what they really care about is, do you love them.

From Rev. Dr. David A. Farmer, senior minister of Silverside Church, Wilmington, Delaware, and longtime editor of *Pulpit Digest:*

1. As parishioners and staff members tend to read initial behaviors as permanent ones, be certain that what you do early in your pastorate is what you want to be doing for the rest of it.

2. Always express heartfelt respect for your church's past while demonstrating that "new and different" can be wonderful too.

3. Make it clear from the outset that you have a life with significant people in it and that you must nurture personal relationships as well as public ones.

4. Meet as soon as possible with the pastor/parish committee (or whatever corresponds to it in your church) for an upbeat, thorough conversation about the congregation's needs and expectations. Among other things to define at this meeting are known problems in the congregation or among the staff and what to do when there are problems.

5. As you are committed to high standards of preaching and worship, let it be known generally in the church what your study needs and habits are, so that people will recognize how serious you are about this aspect of ministry.

6. Let people know through your preaching what your vision for the church is and what your level of self-understanding is. Be personable and confessional in preaching, but not self-centered and narcissistic.

7. Make it understood that you need continuing study and reflection to grow as a pastor, and that you will gratefully accept any and all opportunities for continuing education.

8. Determine from the beginning what your own support options are. Is there a ministerial alliance in the community? On whom would you call if you found yourself in need of a therapist?

9. Meet personally with every member of the staff to discuss your mutual visions for the church and how you can best operate as a leader in their midst.

10. Waste no time in learning the lay of the land in your pastorate. Become acquainted with hospitals, retirement homes, and various assistance organizations that will amplify and undergird your own ministry.

From Rev. Dr. K. Thomas Greene, retired former minister of Triangle Baptist Church, Raleigh, North Carolina:

1. Take the gospel seriously, but not yourself.

2. Read the writers whose points of view differ from yours.

3. Keep handy notes on everything you see, hear, and read.

4. Preach and teach as if someone's soul depends on what you say; it does.

5. Join or form an ecumenical group of pastors in your community.

6. Don't be so heavenly minded that you are of no earthly use.

7. Learn who the power brokers in your church are and get to know them well; it will be time well spent.

8. Bathe every sermon in prayer before you preach it.

9. Have a good sense of humor, but don't be so humorous in the pulpit that people wonder if they have stumbled into a comedy club.

10. Spend real time working on your worship service and the way it flows, because this is when the soul's greatest business is transacted.

From Rev. Dr. Barry Howard, senior minister of First Baptist Church, Pensacola, Florida:

1. Be prepared not only for your Sunday sermons, but also for frequent unexpected, extemporaneous requests as well.

2. Read all you can on a rich variety of subjects, including history, theology, biographies, and novels.

3. Respect diversity. Congregations and communities are growing more and more diverse, so be ready to deal with it.

4. Learn and remember names. There is something about this that communicates to your members that you know and care about them.

5. Don't be afraid to say, "I don't know." People will respect and trust you more if you are willing to admit you don't have all the answers.

6. Be collegial, not competitive. Regard other ministers and churches as your partners in ministry.

7. Maintain confidentiality. Otherwise, you will lose credibility with your congregation.

8. Nurture and maintain friendships outside your congregation. They may prove as rejuvenating as the ones inside your congregation prove to be demanding and draining.

9. Stay marketable outside of ministry. Even if you never have to leave the ministry, having somewhere else to go will give you an added sense of freedom and self-confidence.

10. Leave well. Regardless of why you may be transferring to another place of service, always depart with class and gratitude.

From Rev. Dr. Robert Hundley, senior minister of the First United Methodist Church, Mason, Michigan:

1. Be value-centered. Study and practice the biblical and historical values of the Judeo-Christian tradition, and model those values within the community where you are called to serve.

2. Be morally sound, so that how you think and how you behave is always above reproach.

3. Be ethically driven, so that your values and morality exhibit to others the fact that you are, above all, a Christian.

4. Make study and prayer the top priorities of your ministry. Foster in your people a love of the Scriptures and a passion for prayer.

5. Prepare, prepare, prepare. There is no substitute for preparation.

6. Pastors have a lot of influence; use yours wisely. Don't take advantage of the rights and privileges associated with your ordination.

7. Develop an invitational and facilitative style of leadership instead of a dictatorial style. Recruit and then empower staff members and lay leaders with values similar to your own. Be a leader among leaders!

8. Value your people and earn their trust. Visit them frequently and listen to them carefully, so that your tenure in their midst will be both long and productive.

9. Embrace and practice the fruits of the Spirit as outlined in Paul's letter to the Galatians, chapter 5.

10. Bear fruit by growing the church—leading it to spiritual maturity, mission outreach, and service within the community and around the world.

From Rev. Michael W. McCann, priest associate at Grace Episcopal Church, Gainesville, Georgia, and chairman of the Department of History at Lakeview Academy in Gainesville:

1. Don't assume that what you have learned in seminary or from denominational officials has anything to do with what people in an actual parish need and want to receive from your ministry.

2. Remember that it didn't matter in the Gospels what Jesus said, but rather what he *did* in particular with particular people, and that's what ministry is really about: what you do in particular with particular people.

3. Remember that it didn't matter in Paul's epistles what he said, but what he *did* in particular with particular people, too.

4. Read at least three chapters a day in at least three different translations of the Bible. One translation should be from the Jewish Publication Society's *Tanakh*, the Christian Old Testament.

5. Regularly apply what Jesus says about the Pharisees to your own church and your own sermons and teachings.

6. Read contemporary poetry and don't limit yourself to "Christian" poetry. Seek it as a voice like that of the Good Samaritan, the Syro-Phoenician woman, the Centurion, and the man in Paul's dream calling him over into Macedonia, and trust it as a voice calling you and your community outward and deeper into witness and giving to the world.

7. Vote responsibly in all elections, however inconvenient they may be. Prepare to vote by caring about the issues, understanding them, and deciding on them in the context of your own study and experience of the Scriptures and the church community. Call others to do the same without telling them how to think or vote.

8. Actively seek out minority voices in your church and community to come and tell stories of their own Egypt or Exodus experiences.

9. Keep an active prayer life every day, including different kinds of prayer and meditation, even when you receive no answer or comfort.

10. Don't believe in the church. No matter what church authorities say, don't worry about the church. When the church goes out of business, then following Jesus begins.

From Rev. Dr. James McReynolds, licensed mental health practitioner and pastor of First Christian Church, Weeping Water, Nebraska:

1. Have a second competence in medicine, law, education, or anything other than ministry, so you don't feel overly dependent on the religious system of which you're a part.

2. Take care of yourself physically, emotionally, spiritually, and socially in order to spare yourself from burnout, disease, depression, or even early death.

3. Don't hesitate to seek help from a spiritual director or professional practitioner.

4. Maintain healthy and happy relationships with your spouse, children, parents, and grandchildren.

5. Make realistic assessments of your strengths and weaknesses, and let others help you in the areas of weakness.

6. Preach and teach in a manner conducive to congregational health and well-being, always being open to a variety of liturgical and theological styles.

7. Remain radically attuned to God's grace and guidance for your life and ministry.

8. Frequently update your ministry skills, so you remain aware of the latest trends and methods in ministry.

9. Pay attention to ways of leading in meaningful and creative celebration of the sacraments.

10. Seek relationships beyond the church, welcoming diversity and differences into your personal circle of life.

From Rev. Dr. Dwight A. Moody, founding president of the Academy of Preachers:

1. Get a mentor or coach.

2. Travel—especially overseas.

3. Launch a web site.

4. Examine yourself (moods, dispositions, ambitions, handicaps, expectations, etc.).

5. Ask questions (of people, other ministers, of God and the Bible, of your own tradition, etc.).

6. Write—for clarity.

7. Cultivate the imagination (movies, novels, poems, travels, etc.).

8. Make friends.

9. Practice public speaking.

10. Read.

From the Very Reverend Katherine B. Moorehead, dean of St. John's Episcopal Cathedral, Jacksonville, Florida:

1. Love your congregation. If you are there for them in the hospital and genuinely care about their well-being, they will love you back, even if you make a mess of the liturgy and can't preach your way out of a paper bag.

2. Pray daily in a disciplined way. You cannot lead people to do something that you yourself do not do.

3. Tithe your own money to the church. If you do not believe in doing this, no one else will either.

4. Write letters. A short card with a word of encouragement goes a long way.

5. Listen to your people. If people feel heard, they will hang in there, even when you do not do what they want you to do.

6. When making any major change in the church, try it for a season and get people's responses. Trial runs are much less scary than permanent changes.

7. Spend your first year listening to the history and heart of the people of your parish. You cannot lead effectively if you do not know who they are.

8. Find some kind of spiritual direction for yourself and remain in it for as long as you lead a congregation. You must have someone to talk to if you are to counsel others in a healthy way.

9. Learn from the wisdom of a very successful retired pastor or priest who is still happy.

10. Figure out what your strengths are and lean on them, hiring staff members to do the things you don't do well. This requires some humility and insight, but will save you years of pain and inefficiency.

From Rev. Brent Nidiffer, senior minister of First Christian Church, Elizabethton, Tennessee:

1. Try to visit every member of your parish within the first year of becoming their minister. It will build more capital than almost anything else you can do.

2. Keep a record of the names of all the people you meet and review the list at least once a week. Nothing is more magical to people than having the new pastor know their names.

3. Don't succumb to the temptation to try to please everybody all the time. Pleasing God is more important.

4. Weddings are optional, but funerals are essential. If you have to choose between spending time with a grieving family and spending time with some nameless cousin at a wedding, always choose the grieving family.

5. Take any criticism of you and your family seriously, but don't overestimate its impact in the community.

6. Guard your study and prayer time religiously. You can't coast through life on the fumes of your seminary experience.

7. Make your time off a priority and guard it religiously. Exhaustion isn't next to godliness.

8. Include your family in your vocation as well as your vacation.

9. Establish and maintain some definite boundaries in your ministry and communicate these to your parishioners. Otherwise, you'll lose your soul.

10. Always think "we," not "me." You're part of a team, even if you're the senior minister.

From Rev. Paul Prather, Jr., pastor of Bethesda Church (Pentecostal), Mt. Sterling, Kentucky:

1. Meaningful religion is about relationships, not rules.

2. Often, the best thing you can say is nothing. Don't rush to a parishioner who has just lost a loved one and say that God is good or heaven needed another angel. Show up, say "I've very sorry," sit down, and stay a while. It's called "the ministry of presence."

3. Don't dismiss anybody's views until you get to know the person; it will make a difference.

4. You and I aren't as holy as we sometimes think we are, even in a collar.

5. God is far smarter than we are, and God's plans are frequently different from ours.

6. The gospel is the simplest message imaginable, even for ministers: love everybody and forgive everybody, and God will do the same for us.

7. Faith is a journey, not a stopping place.

8. The power of sermons is cumulative; your people will be more affected by the long haul of your ministry than by a few single "great" sermons.

9. Count on the fact that you will be less certain about some things a year from now than you are today, so don't ever assume you already have all the answers.

10. No one—even you—is irreplaceable in the Lord's work.

From Rev. Dr. William R. Russell, retired former senior minister of First Presbyterian Church, Royal Oak, Michigan:

1. From my first seminary field education internship in East Orange, New Jersey: never, when serving Communion, refer to the contents of the Communion cup as "grape juice." I worked for a pastor who did, and every time he lifted the cup, people snickered.

2. From my second seminary field education internship in Red Bank, New Jersey, courtesy of pastor Charlie Webster, who built huge churches in both New Jersey and Florida on this formula: always begin a sermon with a story that will get a laugh, and end with an illustration that will bring a tear.

3. From my Princeton Theological Seminary preaching professor, Dr. Paul Scherer: never—ever!—approach your pulpit unprepared. It is good to rely on the Holy Spirit, but not to the exclusion of one's own work beforehand.

4. From my experience as Bryant Kirkland's first assistant at the Fifth Avenue Presbyterian Church in New York City: if you are a staff member under another minister, never refer to the people in your assigned areas of ministry as "my congregation." The "boss" won't like it!

5. From my first senior pastorate at the Wyoming Presbyterian Church in Millburn, New Jersey: if you inherit an associate who wanted your job, always insist that this person be replaced within six months. Otherwise, that person can make your entire pastorate a living hell.

6. From my decade at the Church of St. Andrew and St. Paul in center-city Montreal: always treat your predecessor with respect. When I insisted that my long-time predecessor in this church be named minister emeritus, those who had loved him immediately loved me as well.

7. From my training for intentional interim ministry with Interim Network in Baltimore, Maryland: all ministries are interims— some intentional and some not. Learn to look backwards and

forwards and to see yourself as a bridge between the past and the future. You are not the be-all and end-all of your church's ministry.

8. From my nine years at the First Presbyterian Church of Deerfield, Illinois: never stay too long in a parish, lest others feel that you have overstayed your welcome and effectiveness. There are few things sadder than pastors being "eased out" because they stayed beyond their "sell-by" dates!

9. From my experience at the First Presbyterian Church of Royal Oak, Michigan: always negotiate everything you really want or care about before you accept a call. Get virtually everything— salary, benefits, allowances, study leave, vacation time, even "perks"—in writing, to avoid misunderstandings and conflicts later.

10. From my chaplaincy of the Black Watch (Royal Highland Regiment) of Canada and our Colonel-in-Chief, Her Majesty Queen Elizabeth, the Queen Mother: "Never stand when one can sit, never sit when one can lie down, and never pass up a chance to go to the bathroom!"

From Rev. Dr. William P. Tuck, retired Southern Baptist pastor; former professor of preaching at Southern Baptist Theological Seminary, Louisville, Kentucky; and 1997 recipient of the Parish Pastor of the Year award from the Academy of Parish Clergy:

1. Focus your ministry on discipling church members and guiding them in spiritual growth.

2. Remember that the boundaries of your congregation's ministry extend far beyond the walls of your church.

3. Help your members become involved in hands-on ministries at all levels—local, national, and international.

4. Pay attention to your own spiritual development. Have a set time and procedure for personal prayer and meditation.

5. Devote at least twenty to twenty-five hours a week to the preparation of solid, biblically based sermons.

6. Be careful not to neglect your own family. Schedule special days and times with them and hold to them without fail, altering them only for personal or pastoral emergencies.

7. Work at developing personal friendships both inside and outside the church.

8. If you have a church staff, learn to work harmoniously with them, mentoring younger members and building a genuine team.

9. As worship is the most central act of a congregation, study carefully to understand what true worship is and to make it deeply meaningful Sunday by Sunday.

10. Review your ministry at regular intervals to correct aberrations and discern ways of improving your overall performance as the pastoral leader.

Other available titles from

Beyond the American Dream
Millard Fuller

In 1968, Millard finished the story of his journey from pauper to millionaire to home builder. His wife, Linda, occasionally would ask him about getting it published, but Millard would reply, "Not now. I'm too busy." This is that story.   978-1-57312-563-5 272 pages/pb **$20.00**

The Black Church
Relevant or Irrelevant in the 21st Century?
Reginald F. Davis

The Black Church contends that a relevant church struggles to correct oppression, not maintain it. How can the black church focus on the liberation of the black community, thereby reclaiming the loyalty and respect of the black community?   978-1-57312-557-4 144 pages/pb **$15.00**

Blissful Affliction
The Ministry and Misery of Writing
Judson Edwards

Edwards draws from more than forty years of writing experience to explore why we use the written word to change lives and how to improve the writing craft.   978-1-57312-594-9 144 pages/pb **$15.00**

Bottom Line Beliefs
Twelve Doctrines All Christians Hold in Common (Sort of)
Michael B. Brown

Despite our differences, there are principles that are bedrock to the Christian faith. These are the subject of Michael Brown's *Bottom Line Beliefs*.   978-1-57312-520-8 112 pages/pb **$15.00**

Christian Civility in an Uncivil World
Mitch Carnell, ed.

When we encounter a Christian who thinks and believes differently, we often experience that difference as an attack on the principles upon which we have built our lives and as a betrayal to the faith. However, it is possible for Christians to retain their differences and yet unite in respect for each other. It is possible to love one another and at the same time retain our individual beliefs.

978-1-57312-537-6 160 pages/pb **$17.00**

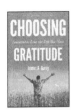

Choosing Gratitude
Learning to Love the Life You Have

James A. Autry

Autry reminds us that gratitude is a choice, a spiritual—not social—process. He suggests that if we cultivate gratitude as a way of being, we may not change the world and its ills, but we can change our response to the world. If we fill our lives with moments of gratitude, we will indeed love the life we have. *978-1-57312-614-4 144 pages/pb* **$15.00**

Contextualizing the Gospel
A Homiletic Commentary on 1 Corinthians

Brian L. Harbour

Harbour examines every part of Paul's letter, providing a rich resource for those who want to struggle with the difficult texts as well as the simple texts, who want to know how God's word—all of it—intersects with their lives today. *978-1-57312-589-5 240 pages/pb* **$19.00**

Dance Lessons
Moving to the Beat of God's Heart

Jeanie Miley

Miley shares her joys and struggles a she learns to "dance" with the Spirit of the Living God. *978-1-57312-622-9 240 pages/pb* **$19.00**

The Disturbing Galilean
Essays About Jesus

Malcolm Tolbert

In this captivating collection of essays, Dr. Malcolm Tolbert reflects on nearly two dozen stories taken largely from the Synoptic Gospels. Those stories range from Jesus' birth, temptation, teaching, anguish at Gethsemane, and crucifixion. *978-1-57312-530-7 140 pages/pb* **$15.00**

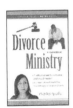

Divorce Ministry
A Guidebook

Charles Qualls

This book shares with the reader the value of establishing a divorce recovery ministry while also offering practical insights on establishing your own unique church-affiliated program. Whether you are working individually with one divorced person or leading a large group, *Divorce Ministry: A Guidebook* provides helpful resources to guide you through the emotional and relational issues divorced people often encounter.

978-1-57312-588-8 156 pages/pb **$16.00**

The Enoch Factor
The Sacred Art of Knowing God
Steve McSwain

The Enoch Factor is a persuasive argument for a more enlightened religious dialogue in America, one that affirms the goals of all religions—guiding followers in self-awareness, finding serenity and happiness, and discovering what the author describes as "the sacred art of knowing God."

978-1-57312-556-7 256 pages/pb **$21.00**

Faith Postures
Cultivating Christian Mindfulness
Holly Sprink

Sprink guides readers through her own growing awareness of God's desire for relationship and of developing the emotional, physical, spiritual postures that enable us to learn to be still, to listen, to be mindful of the One outside ourselves.

1-978-57312-547-5 160 pages/pb **$16.00**

The Good News According to Jesus
A New Kind of Christianity for a New Kind of Christian
Chuck Queen

In *The Good News According to Jesus*, Chuck Queen contends that when we broaden our study of Jesus, the result is a richer, deeper, healthier, more relevant and holistic gospel, a Christianity that can transform this world into God's new world.

978-1-57312-528-4 216 pages/pb **$18.00**

Healing Our Hurts
Coping with Difficult Emotions
Daniel Bagby

In *Healing Our Hurts*, Daniel Bagby identifies and explains all the dynamics at play in these complex emotions. Offering practical biblical insights to these feelings, he interprets faith-based responses to separate overly religious piety from true, natural human emotion. This book helps us learn how to deal with life's difficult emotions in a redemptive and responsible way.

978-1-57312-613-7 144 pages/pb **$15.00**

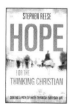

Hope for the Thinking Christian
Seeking a Path of Faith through Everyday Life
Stephen Reese

Readers who want to confront their faith more directly, to think it through and be open to God in an individual, authentic, spiritual encounter will find a resonant voice in Stephen Reese.

978-1-57312-553-6 160 pages/pb **$16.00**

Hoping Liberia
Stories of Civil War from Africa's First Republic
John Michael Helms

Through historical narrative, theological ponderings, personal confession, and thoughtful questions, Helms immerses readers in a period of political turmoil and violence, a devastating civil war, and the immeasurable suffering experienced by the Liberian people.

978-1-57312-544-4 208 pages/pb **$18.00**

A Hungry Soul Desperate to Taste God's Grace
Honest Prayers for Life
Charles Qualls

Part of how we *see* God is determined by how we *listen* to God. There is so much noise and movement in the world that competes with images of God. This noise would drown out God's beckoning voice and distract us. We may not sense what spiritual directors refer to as the *thin place*—God come near. Charles Qualls's newest book offers readers prayers for that journey toward the meaning and mystery of God.

978-1-57312-648-9 152 pages/pb **$14.00**

James (Smyth & Helwys Annual Bible Study series)
Being Right in a Wrong World
Michael D. McCullar

Unlike Paul, who wrote primarily to congregations defined by Gentile believers, James wrote to a dispersed and persecuted fellowship of Hebrew Christians who would soon endure even more difficulty in the coming years.

Teaching Guide 1-57312-604-5 160 pages/ pb **$14.00**

Study Guide 1-57312-605-2 96 pages/pb **$6.00**

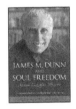

James M. Dunn and Soul Freedom
Aaron Douglas Weaver

James Milton Dunn, over the last fifty years, has been the most aggressive Baptist proponent for religious liberty in the United States. Soul freedom—voluntary, uncoerced faith and an unfettered individual conscience before God—is the basis of his understanding of church-state separation and the historic Baptist basis of religious liberty.

978-1-57312-590-1 224 pages/pb **$18.00**

To order call **1-800-747-3016** or visit **www.helwys.com**

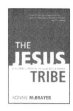
The Jesus Tribe
Following Christ in the Land of the Empire
Ronnie McBrayer

The Jesus Tribe fleshes out the implications, possibilities, contradictions, and complexities of what it means to live within the Jesus Tribe and in the shadow of the American Empire.

978-1-57312-592-5 208 pages/pb **$17.00**

Joint Venture
Jeanie Miley

Joint Venture is a memoir of the author's journey to find and express her inner, authentic self, not as an egotistical venture, but as a sacred responsibility and partnership with God. Miley's quest for Christian wholeness is a rich resource for other seekers.

978-1-57312-581-9 224 pages/pb **$17.00**

Let Me More of Their Beauty See
Reading Familiar Verses in Context
Diane G. Chen

Let Me More of Their Beauty See offers eight examples of how attention to the historical and literary settings can safeguard against taking a text out of context, bring out its transforming power in greater dimension, and help us apply Scripture appropriately in our daily lives.

978-1-57312-564-2 160 pages/pb **$17.00**

Looking Around for God
The Strangely Reverent Observations of an Unconventional Christian
James A. Autry

Looking Around for God, Autry's tenth book, is in many ways his most personal. In it he considers his unique life of faith and belief in God. Autry is a former Fortune 500 executive, author, poet, and consultant whose work has had a significant influence on leadership thinking.

978-157312-484-3 144 pages/pb **$16.00**

Maggie Lee for Good
Jinny and John Hinson

Maggie Lee for Good captures the essence of a young girl's boundless faith and spirit. Her parents' moving story of the accident that took her life will inspire readers who are facing loss, looking for evidence of God's sustaining grace, or searching for ways to make a meaningful difference in the lives of others.

978-1-57312-630-4 144 pages/pb **$15.00**

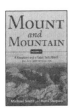

Mount and Mountain
Vol. 1: A Reverend and a Rabbi Talk About the Ten Commandments
Rami Shapiro and Michael Smith

Mount and Mountain represents the first half of an interfaith dialogue—a dialogue that neither preaches nor placates but challenges its participants to work both singly and together in the task of reinterpreting sacred texts. Mike and Rami discuss the nature of divinity, the power of faith, the beauty of myth and story, the necessity of doubt, the achievements, failings, and future of religion, and, above all, the struggle to live ethically and in harmony with the way of God. *978-1-57312-612-0 144 pages/pb* **$15.00**

Overcoming Adolescence
Growing Beyond Childhood into Maturity
Marion D. Aldridge

In *Overcoming Adolescence*, Marion Aldridge poses questions for adults of all ages to consider. His challenge to readers is one he has personally worked to confront: to grow up *all the way*—mentally, physically, academically, socially, emotionally, and spiritually. The key involves not only knowing how to work through the process but also how to recognize what may be contributing to our perpetual adolescence.

978-1-57312-577-2 156 pages/pb **$17.00**

Psychic Pancakes & Communion Pizza
More Musings and Mutterings of a Church Misfit
Bert Montgomery

Psychic Pancakes & Communion Pizza is Bert Montgomery's highly anticipated follow-up to *Elvis, Willie, Jesus & Me* and contains further reflections on music, film, culture, life, and finding Jesus in the midst of it all. *978-1-57312-578-9 160 pages/pb* **$16.00**

Reading Job (Reading the Old Testament series)
A Literary and Theological Commentary
James L. Crenshaw

At issue in the Book of Job is a question with which most all of us struggle at some point in life, "Why do bad things happen to good people?" James Crenshaw has devoted his life to studying the disturbing matter of theodicy—divine justice—that troubles many people of faith.

978-1-57312-574-1 192 pages/pb **$22.00**

To order call **1-800-747-3016** or visit **www.helwys.com**

Reading Samuel (Reading the Old Testament series)
A Literary and Theological Commentary
Johanna W. H. van Wijk-Bos

Interpreted masterfully by preeminent Old Testament scholar Johanna W. H. van Wijk-Bos, the story of Samuel touches on a vast array of subjects that make up the rich fabric of human life. The reader gains an inside look at leadership, royal intrigue, military campaigns, occult practices, and the significance of religious objects of veneration.

978-1-57312-607-6 272 pages/pb **$22.00**

The Role of the Minister in a Dying Congregation
Lynwood B. Jenkins

In *The Role of the Minister in a Dying Congregation* Jenkins provides a courageous and responsible resource on one of the most critical issues in congregational life: how to help a congregation conclude its ministry life cycle with dignity and meaning.

978-1-57312-571-0 96 pages/pb **$14.00**

Sessions with Philippians (Session Bible Studies series)
Finding Joy in Community
Bo Prosser

In this brief letter to the Philippians, Paul makes clear the centrality of his faith in Jesus Christ, his love for the Philippian church, and his joy in serving both Christ and their church.

978-1-57312-579-6 112 pages/pb **$13.00**

Sessions with Samuel (Session Bible Studies series)
Stories from the Edge
Tony W. Cartledge

In these stories, Israel faces one crisis after another, a people constantly on the edge. Individuals such as Saul and David find themselves on the edge as well, facing troubles of leadership and personal struggle. Yet, each crisis becomes a gateway for learning that God is always present, that hope remains.

978-1-57312-555-0 112 pages/pb **$13.00**

Silver Linings
My Life Before and After Challenger 7
June Scobee Rodgers

We know the public story of *Challenger 7*'s tragic destruction. That day, June's life took a new direction that ultimately led to the creation of the Challenger Center and to new life and new love. Her story of Christian faith and triumph over adversity will inspire readers of every age.

978-1-57312-570-3 352 pages/hc **$28.00**

Spacious
Exploring Faith and Place
Holly Sprink

Exploring where we are and why that matters to God is an incredible, ongoing process. If we are present and attentive, God creatively and continuously widens our view of the world, whether we live in the Amazon or in our own hometown.

978-1-57312-649-6 156 pages/pb **$16.00**

This Is What a Preacher Looks Like
Sermons by Baptist Women in Ministry
Pamela Durso, ed.

In this collection of sermons by thirty-six Baptist women, their voices are soft and loud, prophetic and pastoral, humorous and sincere. They are African American, Asian, Latina, and Caucasian. They are sisters, wives, mothers, grandmothers, aunts, and friends.

978-1-57312-554-3 144 pages/pb **$18.00**

To Be a Good and Faithful Servant
The Life and Work of a Minister
Cecil Sherman

This book offers a window into how one pastor navigated the many daily challenges and opportunities of ministerial life and shares that wisdom with church leaders wherever they are in life—whether serving as lay leaders or as ministers just out of seminary, midway through a career, or seeking renewal after many years of service.

978-1-57312-559-8 208 pages/pb **$20.00**

Transformational Leadership
Leading with Integrity
Charles B. Bugg

"Transformational" leadership involves understanding and growing so that we can help create positive change in the world. This book encourages leaders to be willing to change if they want to help transform the world. They are honest about their personal strengths and weaknesses, and are not afraid of doing a fearless moral inventory of themselves.

978-1-57312-558-1 112 pages/pb **$14.00**

Written on My Heart
Daily Devotions for Your Journey through the Bible
Ann H. Smith

Smith takes readers on a fresh and exciting journey of daily readings of the Bible that will change, surprise, and renew you.

978-1-57312-549-9 288 pages/pb **$18.00**

When Crisis Comes Home
Revised and Expanded

John Lepper

The Bible is full of examples of how God's people, with homes grounded in the faith, faced crisis after crisis. These biblical personalities and families were not hopeless in the face of catastrophe—instead, their faith in God buoyed them, giving them hope for the future and strength to cope in the present. John Lepper will help you and your family prepare for, deal with, and learn from crises in your home.   *978-1-57312-539-0 152 pages/pb* **$17.00**

Cecil Sherman Formations Commentary
Add the wit and wisdom of Cecil Sherman to your library. He wrote the Smyth & Helwys Formations Commentary for 15 years; now you can purchase the 5-volume compilation covering the best of Cecil Sherman from Genesis to Revelation.

Vol. 1: Genesis–Job   *1-57312-476-1 208 pages/pb* **$17.00**

Vol. 2: Psalms–Malachi   *1-57312-477-X 208 pages/pb* **$17.00**

Vol. 3: Matthew–Mark   *1-57312-478-8 208 pages/pb* **$17.00**

Vol. 4: Luke–Acts   *1-57312-479-6 208 pages/pb* **$17.00**

Vol. 5: Romans–Revelation   *1-57312-480-X 208 pages/pb* **$17.00**

Made in the USA
Charleston, SC
17 April 2013